zusammengestellt von Dietrich Kessler

KDM
VERLAG

Tel. (0 30) 2 16 34 97, Fax (0 30) 2 16 33 24
Gestaltung: Nele Ellerich
Druck: Kupijai & Prochnow, Berlin
Printed in Germany
ISBN 3-927503-38-X
ISMN M-700065-12-6
Bestell-Nr. 20984-39

INHALT

Dietrich Kessler
Einstieg ins Gitarrenspiel
exclusiv
mit Noten, Tabulaturen und CD
Akkordgriffe - Begleitrhythmen
Blues & Rock Patterns
Power Chords - Übungen - Songs

ABSOLUTE Beginners

Musik und Text:
David Bowie
Interpret: David Bowie
Rhythmus: Rock
Tempo: Moderato

C Hm Em A
but I'm ab- so- lute- ly same.
with no- thing much atstake.
D Hm
As long as we to- ge- ther,
As long as you'restill smil-ing,
Amaj7 G° F#7-9
the rest can go to hell.
there's no- thing more I need.
G G6 D
I ab- so- lute- ly love you,
I ab- so- lute- ly love you,
C Hm
but we're ab- so- lute be- gin- ners
but we're ab- so- lute be- bin- ners.

G D
with eyes com- plete- ly o- pen,
But if my love is your love
F# A G/A A
but ner- vous all the same. If our
we're cer- tain not suc- ceed. If our
D G
love song could fly o- ver moun- tains;
love song could fly o- ver moun- tains;
Hm
could laugh at the o- cean just like the
could sail o- ver heart- aches just like the
F# Em A D
films, there's no rea- son
films, if there's rea- son

G
to feel all the hard times, to lay down the
to feel all the hard times, to lay down the
Hm A G/A
1.
hard lines. It's ab- so- lute- ly true.
hard lines. It's ab- so- lute
A D
2.
(instr.)
ly true.
G Hm
F# Em A Asus4 A
1.3
2.4
repeat and fade

All Around The World

Musik und Text: Lisa Stansfield / Ian Devaney / Andy Morris
Interpretin: Lisa Stansfield
Rhythmus: Pop
Tempo: Moderato

Am7
Em7 A7
but I'm gon- na find him.
Gm9
C
We had a quar- rel and I let my- self go.
Fmaj7
Dm7
I said so ma- ny things, things he did- n't know, and
C
Fmaj7
Em7 A7
1.
I was so, oh, so bad. I don't think he's com- ing back.
Dm7
2.
Asus4
F#m7
I did too much ly- ing, wast- ed too much time.

A7sus4
F#m7 A7sus4 Gm9
Now I'm here I'm cry-ing.
Been a- round the world and I I I
C
Gm9
I can't find my ba- by.
I don't know when, I don't know why,
C
Am7
why he's gave a- way, and I don't know where he can be,
B♭maj7
Am7
Em7 A7
my ba- by,
but I'm gon- na find him.
B♭maj7
C

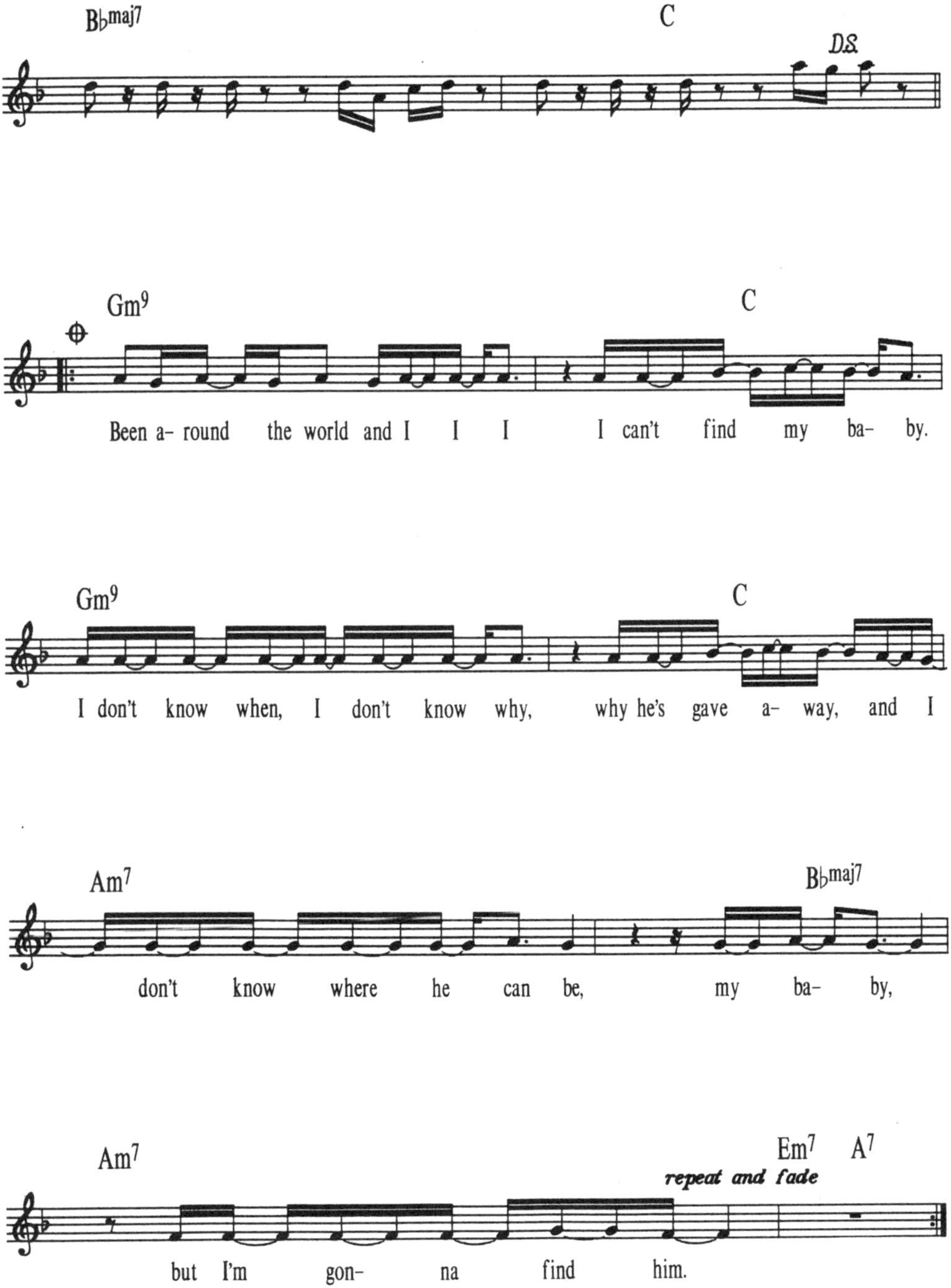
B♭maj7
C
D.S.
Gm9
C
Been a- round the world and I I I I can't find my ba- by.
Gm9
C
I don't know when, I don't know why, why he's gave a- way, and I
Am7
B♭maj7
don't know where he can be, my ba- by,
Am7
Em7 A7
repeat and fade
but I'm gon- na find him.

ALOHA OHE

Traditional
Rhythmus: Latin
Tempo: Moderato

G A7 D G D
a hi-hi le hua of the vale. Fare- well to thee, fare- well to thee. Thou
A D G
charm- ing one who dwells a- mong the bow- ers. One found em- brace be-
D A7 D
fore I know de- part un- til we meet a- gain.

Alouette

Volkslied aus Frankreich
Tempo: Allegro

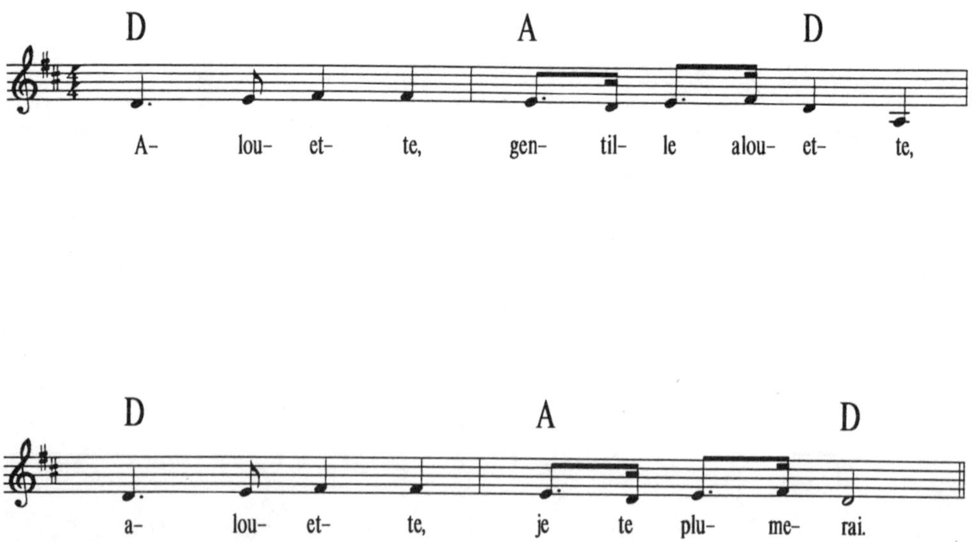

D A7 D
1. Je te plu- me- rai la tet', je te plu- me- rai la tet',
2. Je te plu- me- rai le coup, je te plu- me- rai le coup,
3. Je te plu- me- rai les ailes, je te plu- me- rai les ailes,
4. Je te plu- me- rai les pattes, je te plu- me- rai les pattes,
5. Je te plu- me- rai le dos, je te plu- me- rai le dos,
6. Je te plu- me- rai la queue, je te plu- me- rai la queue,
et la tet', et la tet', et la tet', et la tet'.
et la tet', et la tet', et le coup, et le coup,
et les ailes, et le coup, et la tet', et la tet',
et les pattes, et les ailes, et le coup, et la tet',
et le dos, et les ailes, et le coup, et la tet',
et les pattes, et les ailes, et le coup, et la tet',
D
A- lou- et', a- lou- et', ah!

Angie

Musik und Text:
Mick Jagger / Keith Richard
Interpreten: Rolling Stones
Rhythmus: Rock Ballade
Tempo: Slow

2. Angie, you're beautiful, but ain't it time we said goodbye. Angie, I still love you, remember all those nights we cried.
All the dreams we held so close seemed to all go up in smoke, let me whisper in your ear, Angie, Angie, where will it lead us from here.

3. INSTRUMENTAL ... Oh Angie don't you weep, ah, your kisses still taste sweet,
I hate theat sadness in your eyes. But Angie, Angie, ain't it time we said goodbye.

4. INSTRUMENTAL ... With no loving in our souls and no money in our coats, you can't say we're satisfied. But Angie, I still love you baby,
Ev'rywhere I look I see your eyes. There ain't a woman that comes close to you, come on baby dry ypur eyes.

Ain't She Sweet

Musik: Milton Ager
Text: Jack Yellen
Interpret: Gene Vincent
Rhythmus: Swing
Tempo: Moderato

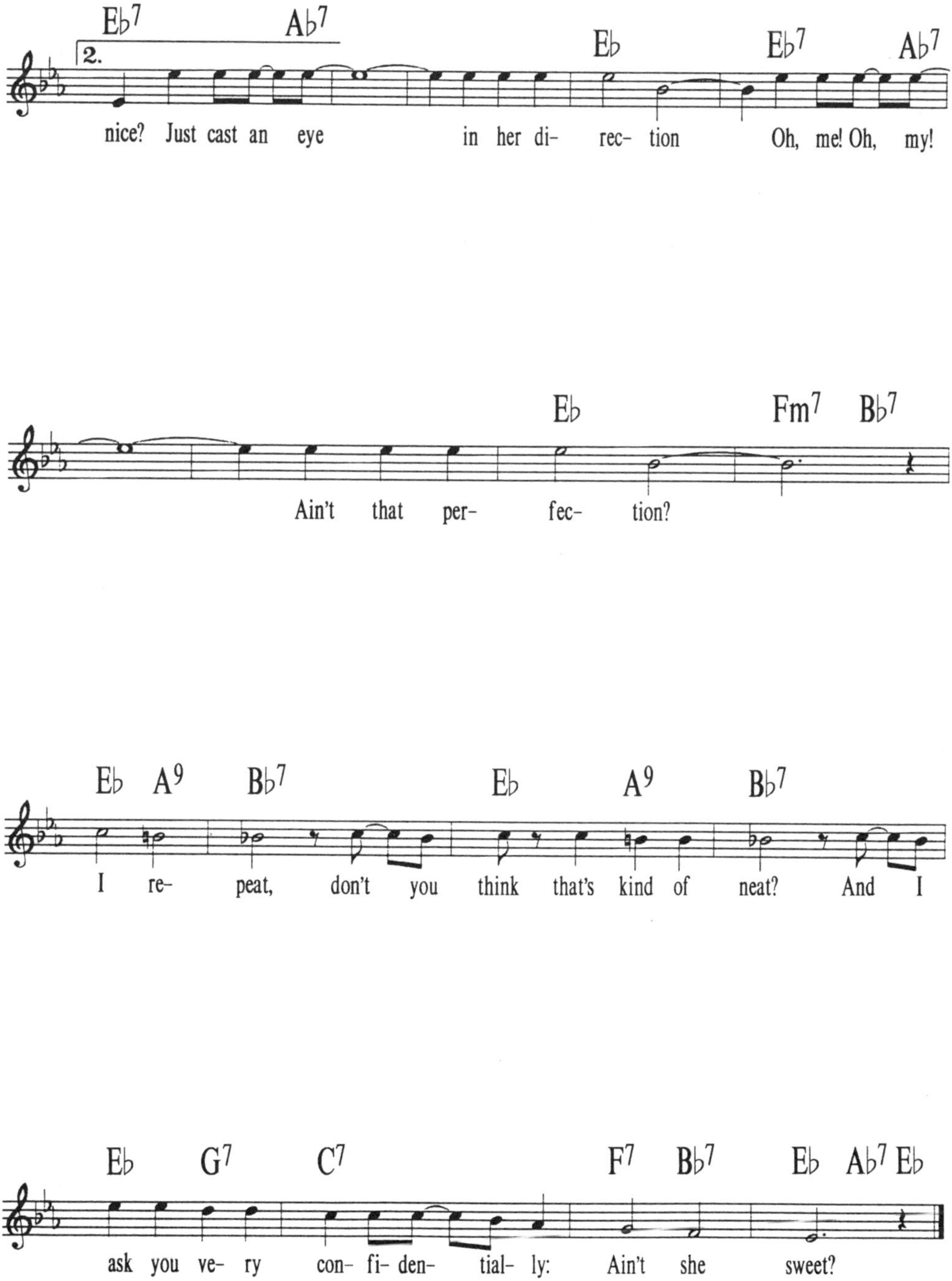
Eb7 Ab7 Eb Eb7 Ab7
2.
nice? Just cast an eye in her di- rec- tion Oh, me! Oh, my!
Eb Fm7 Bb7
Ain't that per- fec- tion?
Eb A9 Bb7 Eb A9 Bb7
I re- peat, don't you think that's kind of neat? And I
Eb G7 C7 F7 Bb7 Eb Ab7 Eb
ask you ve- ry con- fi- den- tial- ly: Ain't she sweet?

BANKS OF THE OHIO

Traditional
Interpretin: Olivia Newton-John
Rhythmus: Ballade
Tempo: Moderato

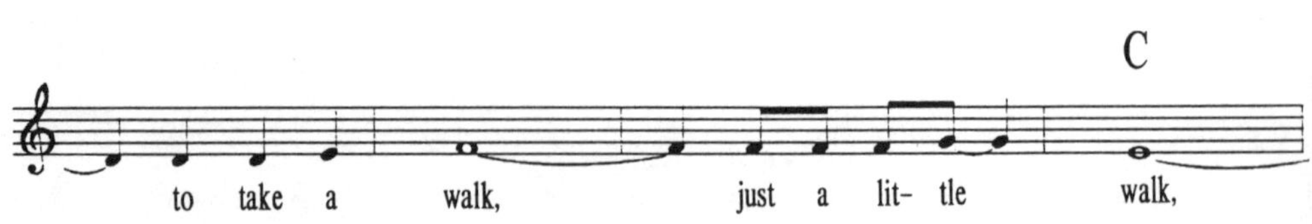

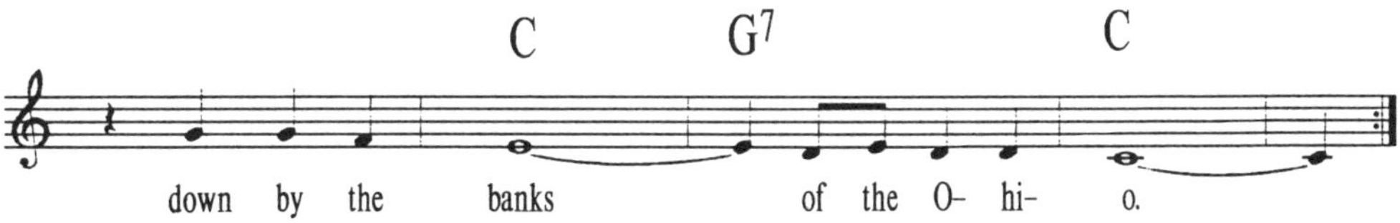

2. I held a knife against her breast
As into my arms she pressed,
She cried: "Oh, Willie, don't murder me,
I'm not prepared for eternity."
And only say that you'll be mine,
In no others arms entwine,
Down beside where the waters flow,
Down by the banks of the Ohio

3. I started home 'tween twelfe and one,
I cried: "My God! What have I done?
Killed the only woman I loved,
Because she would not be my bride."
And only say that you'll be mine,
In no others arms entwine,
Down beside where the waters flow,
Down by the banks of the Ohio

VENUS

Musik und Text:
Rob van Leeuwen
Interpreten: Shocking Blue
Rhythmus: Rock
Tempo: Moderato

Am D Em A Em A C
Yeah, ba- by, she's got it! Well, I'm your Ve-nus,
H4 Em A Em A
I'm your fi- re at your de- sire. Well,
C H4 Em A Em A
I'm your Ve-nus, I'm your fi-re at your de-sire.
Em A
1.
Em A
2
D.C.
Em A Em A
Em A Em A Em
1.
2.
She's

verdammt, ich lieb' dich

Musik und Text:
Bernd Dietrich / Matthias Reim
Interpret: Matthias Reim
Rhythmus: Pop
Tempo: Moderato

2. So langsam fällt mir alles wieder ein: ich wollt' doch nur'n bißchen freier sein.
Jetzt bin ich's, oder nicht? Ich paßte nicht in deine heile Welt,
Doch die und du ist, was mir jetzt so fehlt, ich glaub' das einfach nicht!
Gegenüber steht ein Telefon, es lacht mich ständig an voll Hohn,
Es klingelt, klingelt aber nicht. Sieben Bier, zuviel geraucht,
Das ist es, was ein Mann so braucht, doch niemand, niemand sagt: "Hör' auf!"
Und ich denke schon wieder nur an dich ...

Black Night

Musik und Text: Ritchie Blackmore / Jon Lord / Ian Paice / Ian Gillan / Roger Glover
Interpreten: Deep Purple
Rhythmus: Hard Rock
Tempo: Moderato

I don't fell so bright, I don't care
I don't want a rough sea, I don't feel
I don't need black night, I don't see
N.C.
to sit tight. May- be I'll find on the way down the line that I'm
I can't see
dark night
B♭ A♭ Fm
free. Free to be me. gtr.
B♭ A♭ C
Black night is a long way from home.
Fm
gtr. solo ad lib
N.C. B♭ A♭ Fm
D.S. repeat for fade
no chords
gtr. solo ad lib

BOLLE REISTE JÜNGST ZU PFINGSTEN

Deutsches Volkslied
Tempo: Allegro

2. Zu Pankow gab's kein Essen, zu Pankow gab's kein Bier,
war alles aufgefressen von fremden Leuten hier.
Nicht mal 'ne Butterstulle hat man ihm reserviert,
aber dennoch hat sich Bolle ganz köstlich amüsiert.
Aber dennoch hat sich Bolle ganz köstlich amüsiert.

3. Auf der Schönholzer Heide, da gab's 'ne Keilerei.
Und Bolle, gar nicht feige, war mittenmang dabei,
hat's Messer 'rausgerissen und fünfe massakriert,
aber dennoch hat sich Bolle ganz köstlich amüsiert.
Aber dennoch hat sich Bolle ganz köstlich amüsiert.

4. Es fing schon an zu tagen, als er sein Heim erblickt,
das Hemd war ohne Kragen, das Nasenbein zerknickt,
das linke Auge fehlte, das rechte marmoriert,
aber dennoch hat sich Bolle ganz köstlich amüsiert.
Aber dennoch hat sich Bolle ganz köstlich amüsiert.

5. Zu Hause angekommen, da gings ihm aber schlecht.
Da hat ihn seine Olle ganz mörderisch verdrescht.
'Ne volle halbe Stunde hat sie auf ihm poliert,
aber dennoch hat sich Bolle ganz köstlich amüsiert.
Aber dennoch hat sich Bolle ganz köstlich amüsiert.

6. Bolle wollte sterben, er hat sich's überlegt.
Er hat sich auf die Schienen der Bimmelbahn gelegt.
Die Bahn, die hat Verspätung, und vierzehn Tage drauf
da fand man unsern Bolle als Schimmel wieder auf.
Da fand man unsern Bolle als Schimmel wieder auf.

BROWN SUGAR

Musik und Text:
Mick agger / Keith Richard
Interpreten: Rolling Stones
Rhythmus: Rock
Tempo: Moderato

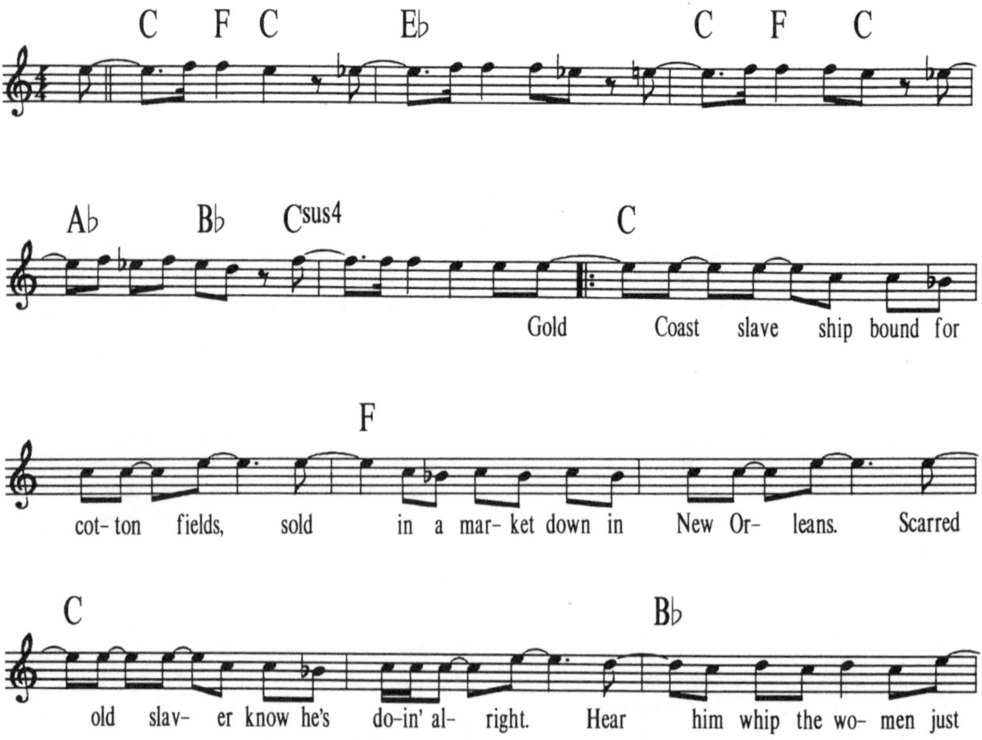

2\. Beating, cold English blood runs hot,
Lady of the house wond'rin' where it's gonna stop.
Houseboy knows that he's doin' alright.
You should aheard him just around midnight.

3\. I bet your mama was a Tent Show queen,
And all her girlfriends were sweet sixteen.
I'm no schoolboy but I know what I like.
You should have heard me just around midnight.

CADILLAC

Musik: K. Brown / D. Gibson / G. Johnson / I. Mallet
Text: Vince Taylor
Rhythmus: Rock
Tempo: Moderato

A7 Em
can't you see I'm on my bend- ed knees,
H7 A7 Em
your heart's so cold that it's gon- na freeze.
H7 Em
Yeah, Ca-dil-lac, oh, Ca-dil- lac,
Am Em
oh, Ca-dil-lac, yeah, Ca-dil- lac,
H7 Am Em
oh, Ca-dil-lac, yeah, Ca-dil- lac.

Come Back Liza

Traditional
Rhythmus: Calypso
Tempo: Moderato

2. I remember when love was new,
Water come to my eye.
There was one but now there is two,
Water come to my eye.
Come back Liza …

3. When the evening start to fall,
Water come to my eye.
I need to hear me Liza come,
Water come to my eye.
Come back Liza …

4. Standing there in the marketplace,
Water come to my eye.
I need to feel the woman breathe,
Water come to my eye.
Come back Liza …

COME PRIMA

Musik: S. Taccini / V. di Paola
Text: M. Panzeri
Rhythmus: Slow Rock
Tempo: Slow

Bb Gm Cm7
pri- ma, co- me pri- ma now I know that in
F7 F7+5 Fm G7
shar- ing love we're touched with heav- en's glow. What a
Cm D7 Gm C7
feel- ing I am feel- ing! For the first time it is true. Co- me
Bb Cm7 F7 Bb Cm7 F7
1.
pri- ma, co- me pri- ma I love you. Co- me
Bb Gm Cm7 F11 F7 Bb Gb Bb6
2.
you. Co-me pri- ma, co-me pri- ma I love you.

CRIMSON and CLOVER

Musik und Text:
Tommy James / Peter Lucia
Rhythmus: Rock Ballade
Tempo: Slow

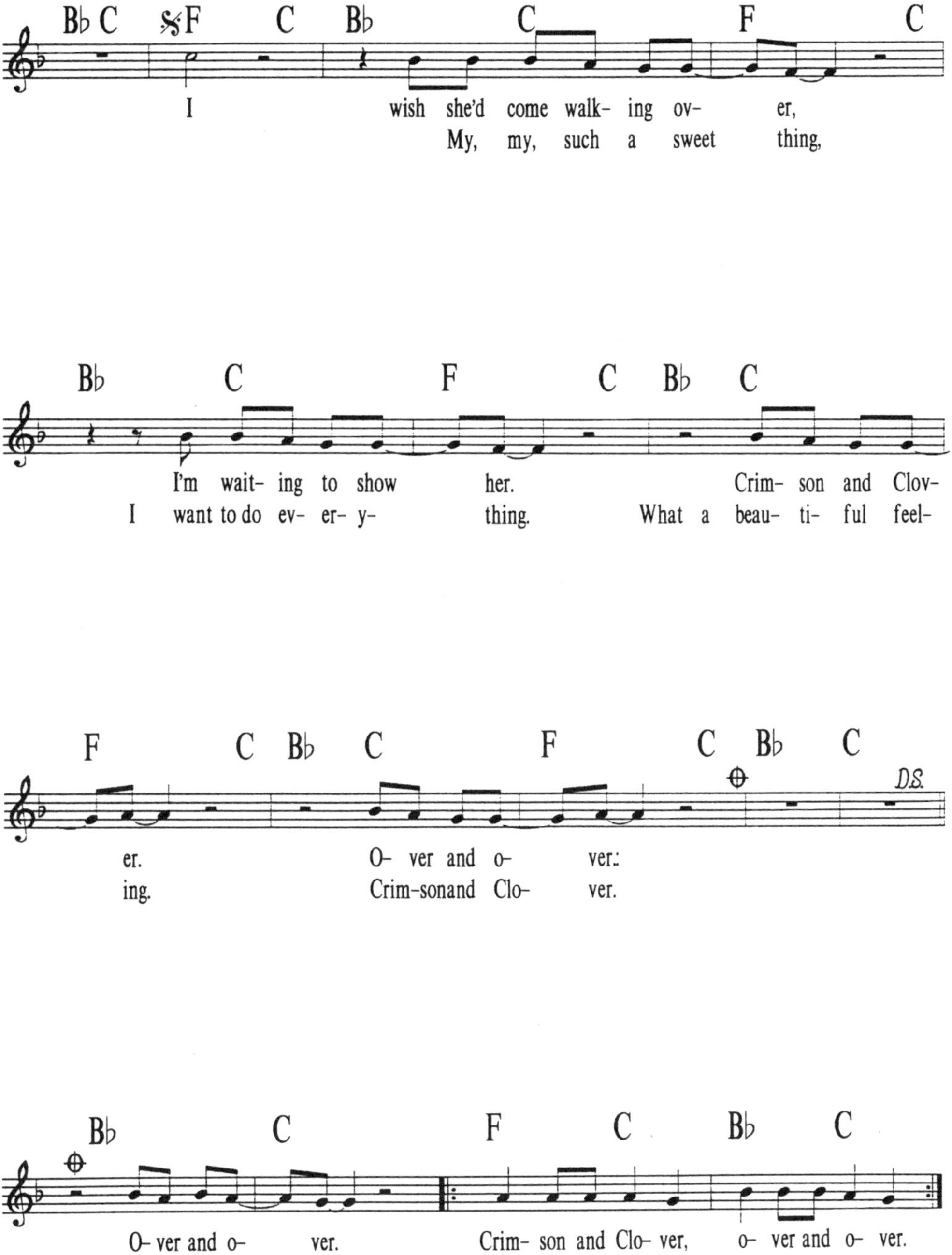
B♭ C 𝄋F C B♭ C F C
I wish she'd come walk- ing ov- er,
My, my, such a sweet thing,
B♭ C F C B♭ C
I'm wait- ing to show her. Crim- son and Clov-
I want to do ev- er- y- thing. What a beau- ti- ful feel-
F C B♭ C F C B♭ C
er. O- ver and o- ver.:
ing. Crim-son and Clo- ver.
D.S.
B♭ C F C B♭ C
O- ver and o- ver. Crim- son and Clo- ver, o- ver and o- ver.

DAT DU MIN LEEVSTEN BÜST

Norddeutsches Volkslied
Rhythmus: Walzer
Tempo: Andante

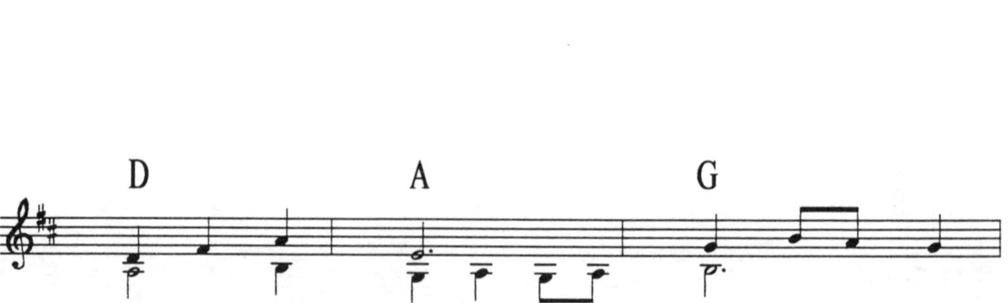

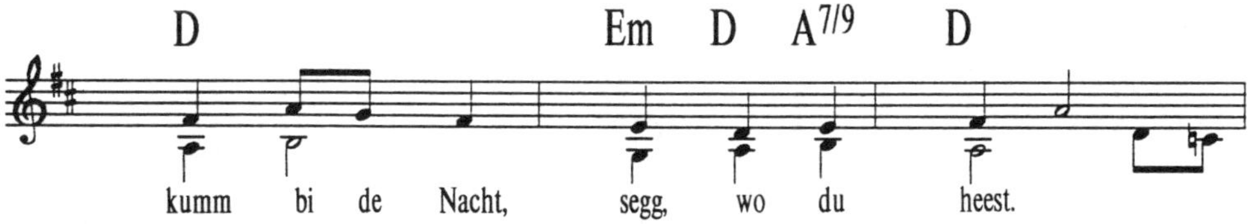

2. Kum du üm Middernacht, kumm du Klock een!
Vader slöpt, Moder slöpt, ick slaap alleen.

3. Klopp an de Kammerdör, fat an de Klink.
Vader meent, Modder meent, dat deit de Wind.

4. Kumm denn de Morgenstund, kreiht de ol Hahn.
Leevster min, Leevster min, denn mößt du gahn.

5. Sachen den Gang henlank, lies mid de Klink!
Vader meent, Moder meent, dat deit de Wind.

DA YA THINK I'M Sexy

Musik und Text:
Rod Stewart / Carmine Appice*
Interpret: Rod Stewart
Rhythmus: Disco Rock
Tempo: Moderato

Dm7
If you real- ly need me, just reach out and touch me. Come
F
on, hon- ey, tell me so.
Gm7 C/B♭ Gm7
He's act- ing shy, look-ing for an an- swer. "Come on, hon- ey, let's
C/B♭ Gm7
spend the night to- geth- er." "Now, hold on a min- ute be-
C/B♭ Gm7 C/B♭
fore we go much fur- ther. Give me a dime, so I can phone my moth- er."

Gm7
C/B♭
Gm7
They catch a cab ti his high- rise ap-part- ment. At last he can tell her ex-
C/B♭
Dm7
act- ly what his heart meant. If you want my bo- dy and
F
you think I'm sex- y, come on, sug- ar, let me know. If
Dm7
you real- ly need me, just reach out and touch me. Come
F
on, hon- ey, tell me so. His

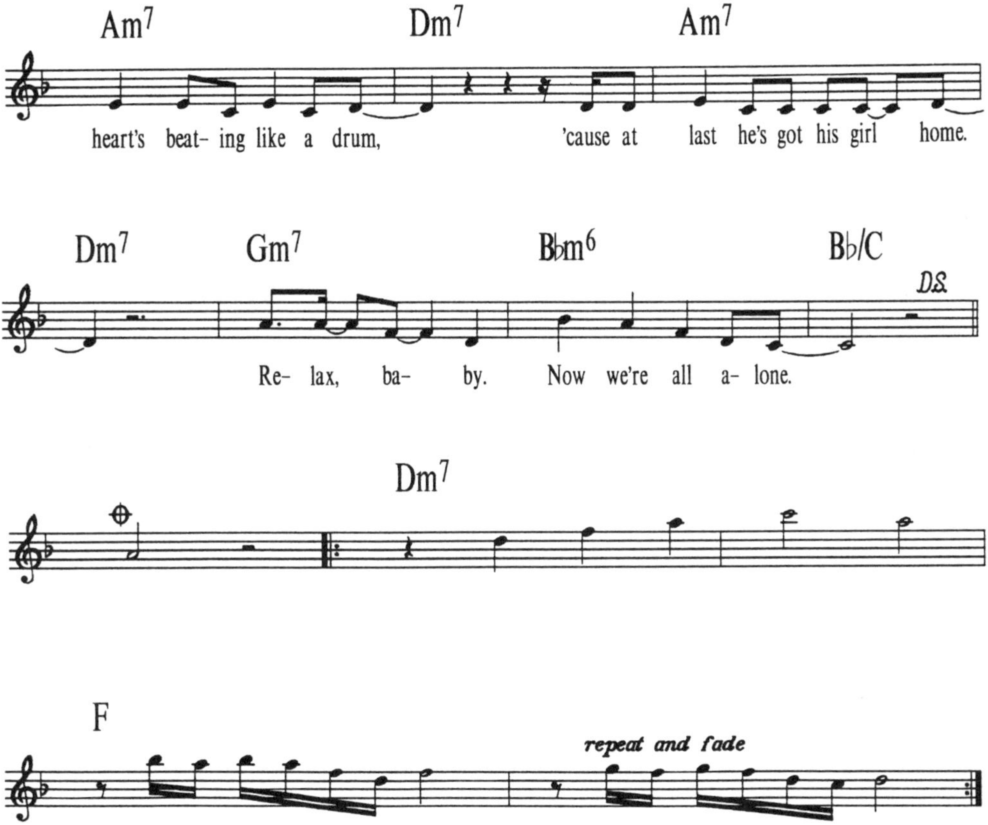

2. They wake at dawn, 'cause all the birds are singing.
Two total strangers, but that ain't what they're thinking!
Outside it's cold, misty and it's raining.
They got each other. Neither one's complaining.
He says, "I'm sorry, but I'm out of milk and coffee."
"Never mind, sugar, we can watch the early movie.

DOWN ON THE CORNER

Musik und Text:
John C. Fogerty
Interpreten: CCR
Rhythmus: Rock
Tempo: Moderato

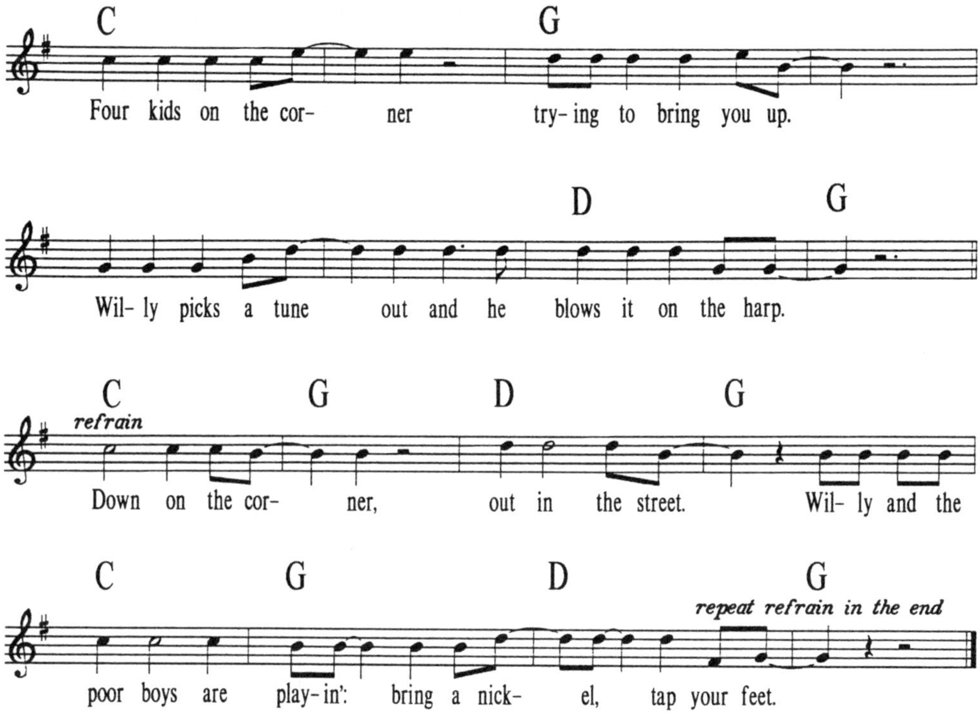

2. Rooster hits the washboard and people just got to smile,
Blinky thumps the gut bass and solos for a while.
Poorboy twangs the rhythm out on his kalomazoo.
Willy goes into a dance and doubles on kazoo.

3. INSTRUMENTAL

4. You don't need a penny just to hang around,
But if you've got a nickel, won't you lay your money down?
Over on the corner there's a happy noise.
People come from all around to watch the magic boys.

EL CHOCLO

Traditional
Rhythmus: Tango Argentine
Tempo: Moderato

Dm C7 F
ff
C7 F A7 Dm
p
Bb7 A A
1. 2.
f p
D A7
mf
D7 H7
Em E7 A
1.
Em E7 A7 D
2.
f

No Milk Today

Musik u. Text: Graham Gouldman
Rhythmus: Rock
Tempo: Moderato

D E7 A Am
Be-hind the door where my love reigned a queen. No milk to-day, It
Be-hind the door where my love reigned a queen. No milk to-day, My
C E7 Am E7
was-n't al-ways so, The com-pan-y was gay, we turned night in-to
love has gone a-way, the bot-tle stands for-lorn, A sym-bol of the
Am A E
day.
dawn.
But all that's left is a
D E A E D F♯m
place dark and lone-ly, A ter-raced house in a mean street back of town,
A E D E D E
Be-comes a shrine when I think of you on-ly. Just two up two down,
1. 2.
Am G Am D9/A
No milk to-day.

EVERYBODY LOVES SATURDAY NIGHT

Traditional
Rhythmus: Swing
Tempo: Moderato

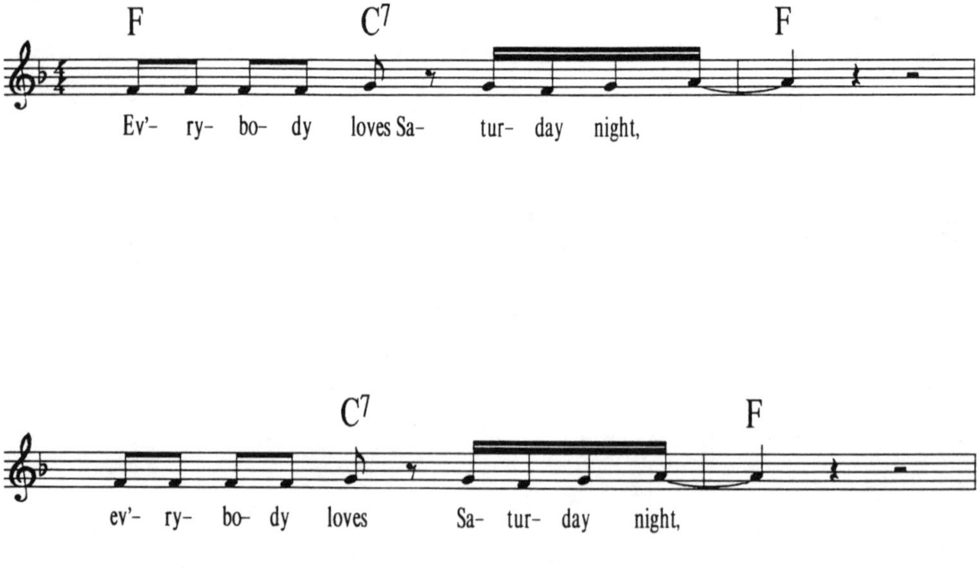

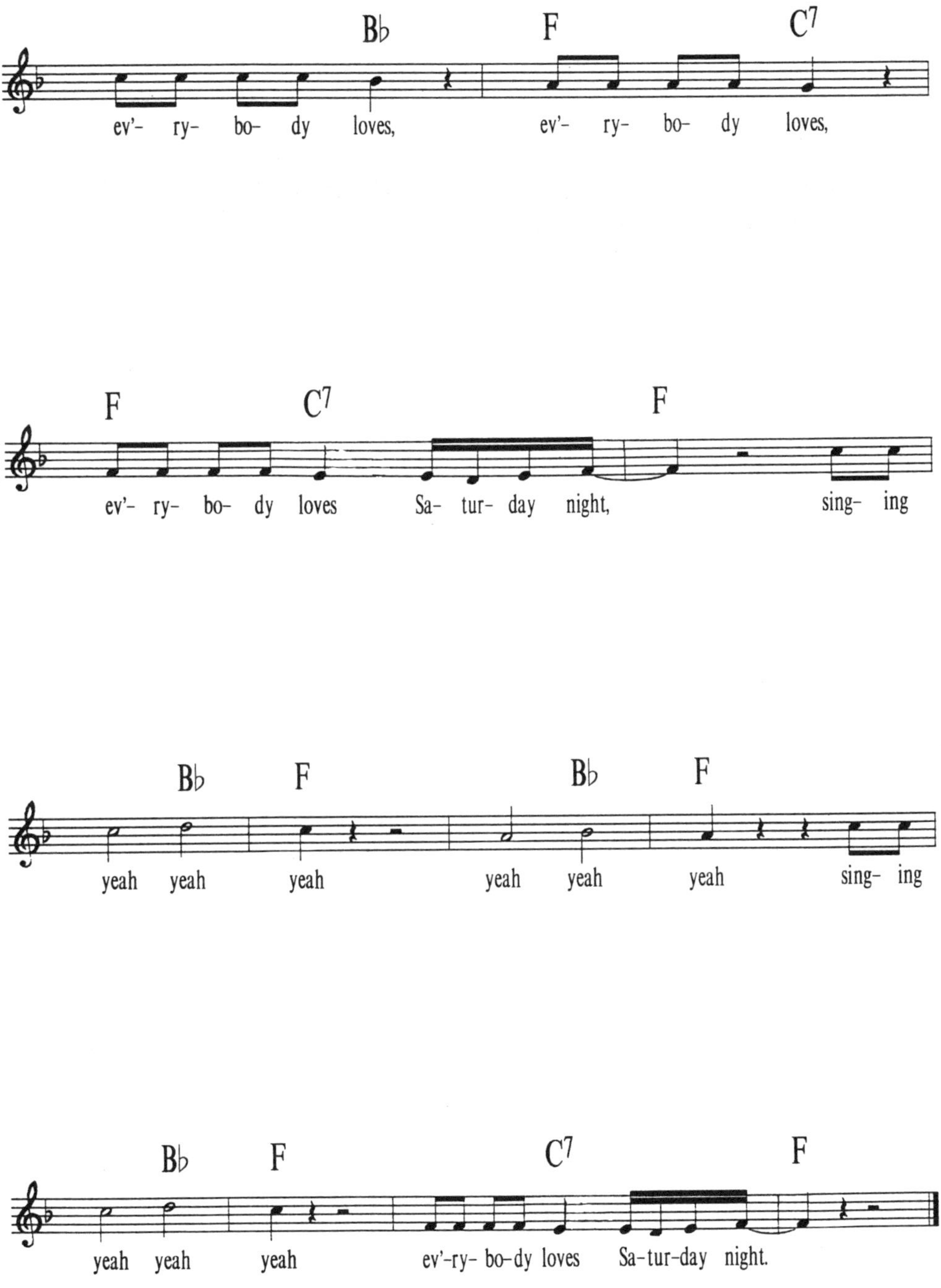
B♭ F C7
ev'- ry- bo- dy loves, ev'- ry- bo- dy loves,
F C7 F
ev'- ry- bo- dy loves Sa- tur- day night, sing- ing
B♭ F B♭ F
yeah yeah yeah yeah yeah yeah sing- ing
B♭ F C7 F
yeah yeah yeah ev'-ry- bo-dy loves Sa-tur-day night.

Everybody Loves Somebody

Musik und Text:
Irving Taylor / Ken Lane
Rhythmus: Medium Swing
Tempo: Slow

2. Ev'rybody finds somebody someplace,
There's no telling where love may appear.
Something in my heart keeps saying
My someplace is now.

3. Ev'rybody loves somebody sometime,
And although my dream was overdue,
Your love made it well worth waiting,
For sometime is now.

Feelings

Musik und Text:
Morris Albert / Lou Gaste
Deutscher Text: Michael Kunze
Tempo: Moderato

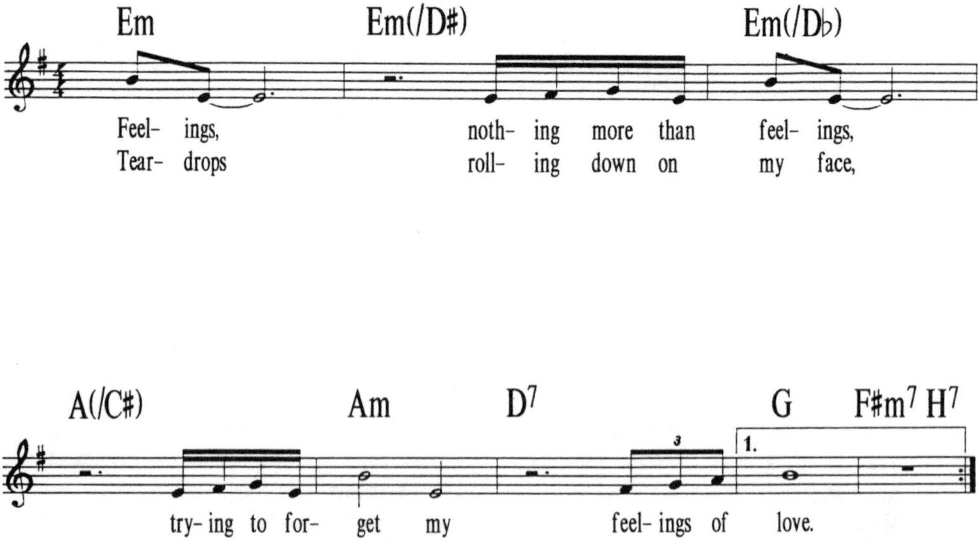

G E7
2.
C Am7 D7 Hm
love. Feel- ings, for all my life I'll feel it.
E7 Am D7 Hm E7
I wish I've nev-er met you girl; you'll nev-er come a- gain.
C Am D7 Hm E7
Feel- ings, wo, wo, wo, feel- ings, wo, wo, wo,
Am D7 Hm7 E7
3
feel you a- gain in my arms.

für Elise

Musik: Ludwig van Beethoven
Classical
Tempo: Moderato

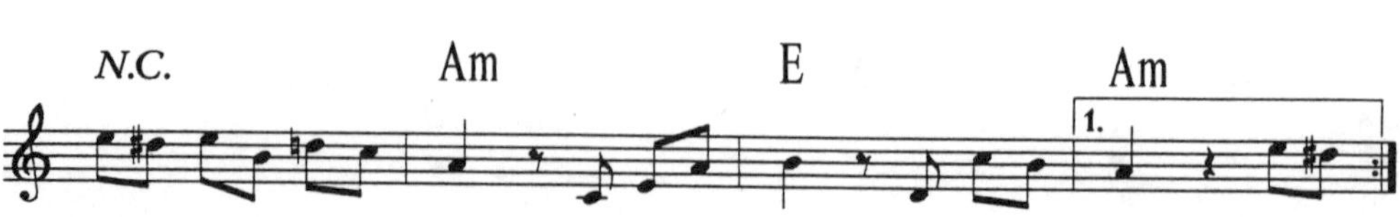

Am C G Am E
2.
N.C. Am E
Am N.C. Am E Am

GLORY LAND

Musik und Text:
Lonnie Donegan
Interpreten: Rattles, The Lords
Rhythmus: Rock
Tempo: Moderato

D (D7) G D7
o- ver in the Glo- ry Land.
G C
Drif- ting thro' life care- less- ly eyes so dimmed I could- n't see
Trou- bles I've got all my own, mean- time gon- na find ahome
G D D7 G
walk- ing to the Glo- ry Land. Sin- ners there are
o-ver in the Glo- ry Land.
C G
rocks a- head de- vils rack- ing in my head. O- ver in the
D7 G G
1. 2.
Glo- ry Land. I'm sing- in' I'm sing- in'

GOODY GOODY

Musik und Text:
Johnny Mercer / MattMalneck
Rhythmus: Swing Rock
Tempo: Brightly

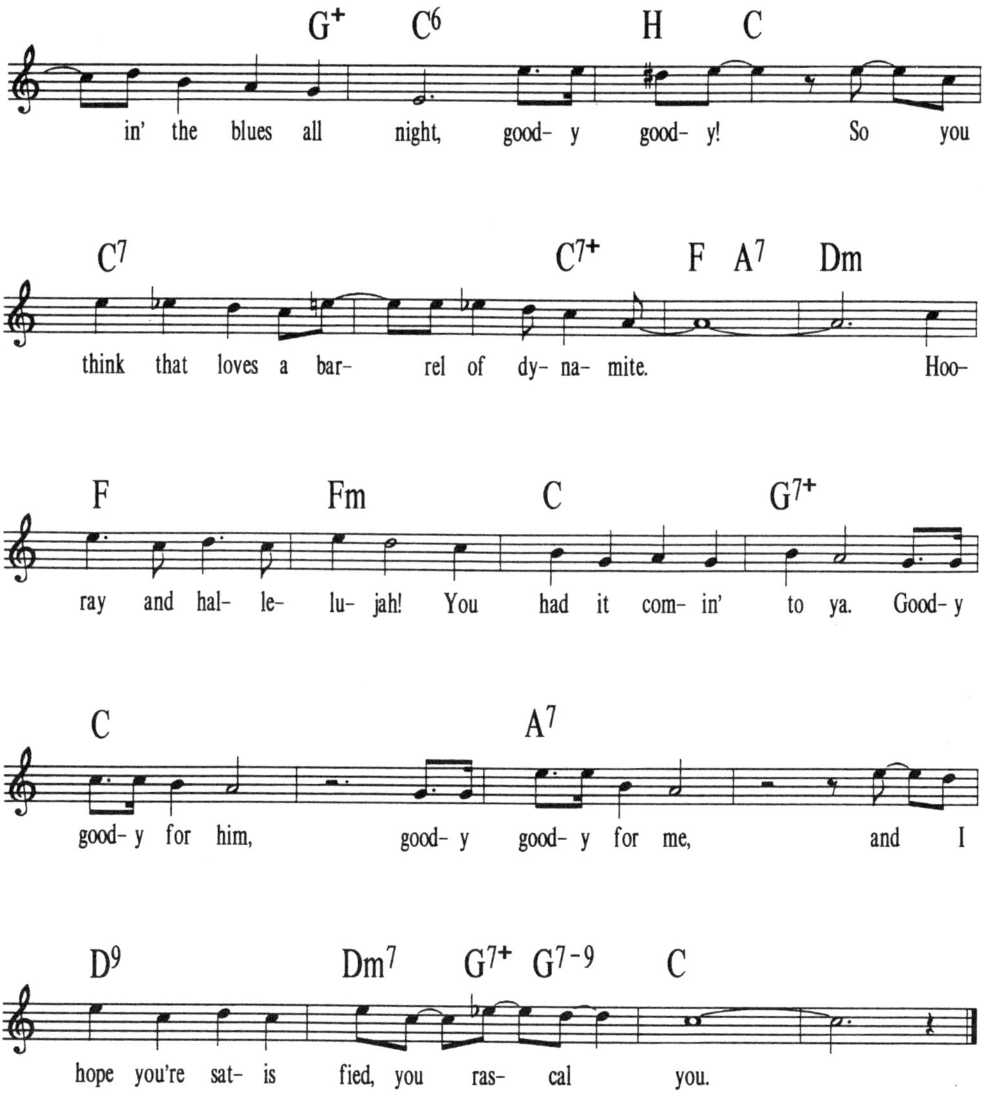
G+ C6 H C
in' the blues all night, good- y good- y! So you
C7 C7+ F A7 Dm
think that loves a bar- rel of dy- na- mite. Hoo-
F Fm C G7+
ray and hal- le- lu- jah! You had it com- in' to ya. Good- y
C A7
good- y for him, good- y good- y for me, and I
D9 Dm7 G7+ G7-9 C
hope you're sat- is fied, you ras- cal you.

Greensleeves

Traditional
Rhythmus: Walzer
Tempo: Allegretto

B♭ A7 Dm G Dm
light- ing in your com- pa- ny.
F Em Am
Green- sleeves was all my joy, and
B♭ Gm A
Green- sleeves was my de- light.
F C
Green- sleeves was my heart of gold and
B♭ A7 Dm G Dm
who but my La- dy Green- sleeves.

Hang On Sloopy

Musik und Text:
Burt Russell / Wes Farrell
Interpreten: Mc Coys
Rhythmus: Rock
Tempo: Moderato

C Bb F Bb C7 Bb F Bb
2.
Come on sloo- py. Come on girl.
C7 Bb F7
Say yeah, yeah, yeah. Good, good, good, good.
F
Good, good, good, good. Oh, I wan- na say Ah.
F7 F
Now I want you to tell me some- thing ba- by.
da capo and fade
F7
Well don't it make you feel cra- zy. I wan- na say Ah.

HAPPY BIRTHDAY

Happy Birthday
Tempo: Moderato

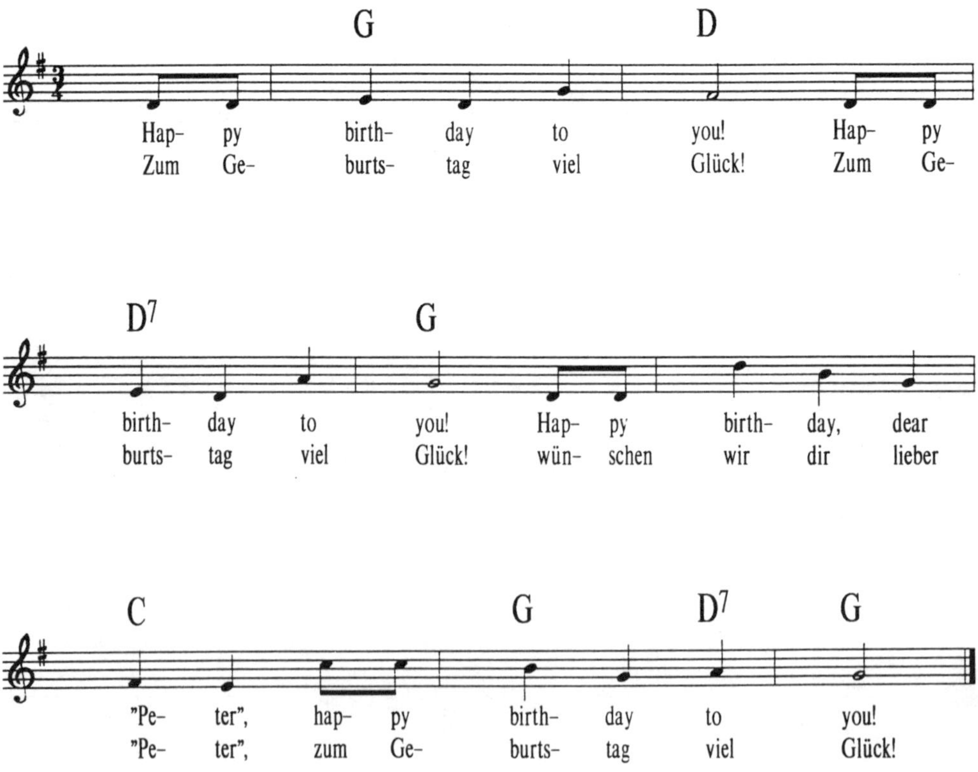

Eve Of Destruction

Musik u. Text: P. F. Sloan
Interpreten: Barry McGuires
Rhythmus: Rock
Tempo: Moderato

D G A7 D G A
1. The Eastern World it is explodin', Violence flarin' an bullets loeadin'.
D G A D
You're old enough to kill, but not for voin'. You don't believe in war,
G A D G A
but what's that gun you're totin'? And even the Jordan River has bodies floatin'!
D G A D Hm
But you tell me over and over and over again my friend.
G A D
Ah, you don't believe we're on the eve of destruction.

2. Don't you understand what I'm try'n to say? Can't you feel the fear
that I'm feelin' to day? If the buttons is pushed there's no running away
there'll be no one to save with the world in a grave.
Take a look around you boy, it's bound to scare you boy,
but you tell me over and over and over again my friend,
Ah, you don't believe we're on the eve of destruction.

3. Yeah, my blood's so mad, feels like coagulation',
I'm sittin' here, just contemplatin', I can't twist the truth,
it knows no regulation, Handful of Senators don't pass legislation,
And marches alone can't bring integration,
When human respect is disintegratin',
This whole crazy world is just too frustration', and you tell me ...

4. Think of all the hate there is in Red China!
Then take a look around to Selma, Alabama! Ah, you may leave here,
for four days in space, but when you return, it's the same old place.
The poundin' of the drums, the pride and disgrace,
You can bury your dead, but don't leave a trace,
Hate your next-door-neighbour, but don't forget to say grace, and you tell me ...

HARLEM SHUFFLE

Musik und Text:
Bob Relf / Earl Nelson
Interpreten: Rolling Stones
Rhythmus: Rock
Tempo: Moderato

You know you scratch just like a mon-key, yeah, you do, real
yeah! You slide in-to the lim-bo, yeah
D7
how low can you go? Oh come on ba- by,
C#m
I don't want you to shuf-fle now you just groove it right

here, to the Har- lem shuf- fle.
C#m
(Girls)Yeah, yeah, yeah do the Har-lem shuf- fle (Boy)Oh do the
mon- key shin- er. (Girls)Yeah, yeah, yeah do the Har-lem shuf-
D7
fle. (Boy)Wa- wa- a- a- a-
C#m
Dm
a- wa.

Dm
Hitch. Hitch-hike ba- by a- cross the floor.
Whoa, whoa, whoa, I can't stand it no more.
Eb7
Now come on ba- by, now get in- to your slide we're gon- na
Dm
ride, ride, ride lit- tle po- ny ride yeah.
Dm
repeat and fade
Shake, shake, shake, shake a tail fea- ther ba- by.

HELLO

Musik und Text:
Lionel Richie
Interpret: Lionel Richie
Rhythmus: Ballade
Tempo: Slow

2. I long to see the sunlight in your hair and tell you time and time again how much I care.
Sometimes I feel my heart will overflow, Hello, I've just got to let you know,
`Cause I wonder where you are and I wonder what you do. Are you somewhere feeling lonely or is someone loving you?
Tell me how to win your heart for I haven't got a clue, but let me start by saying, I love you …

HELLO DOLLY

Musik und Text:
Jerry Herman
Rhythmus: Medium Swing
Tempo: Moderato

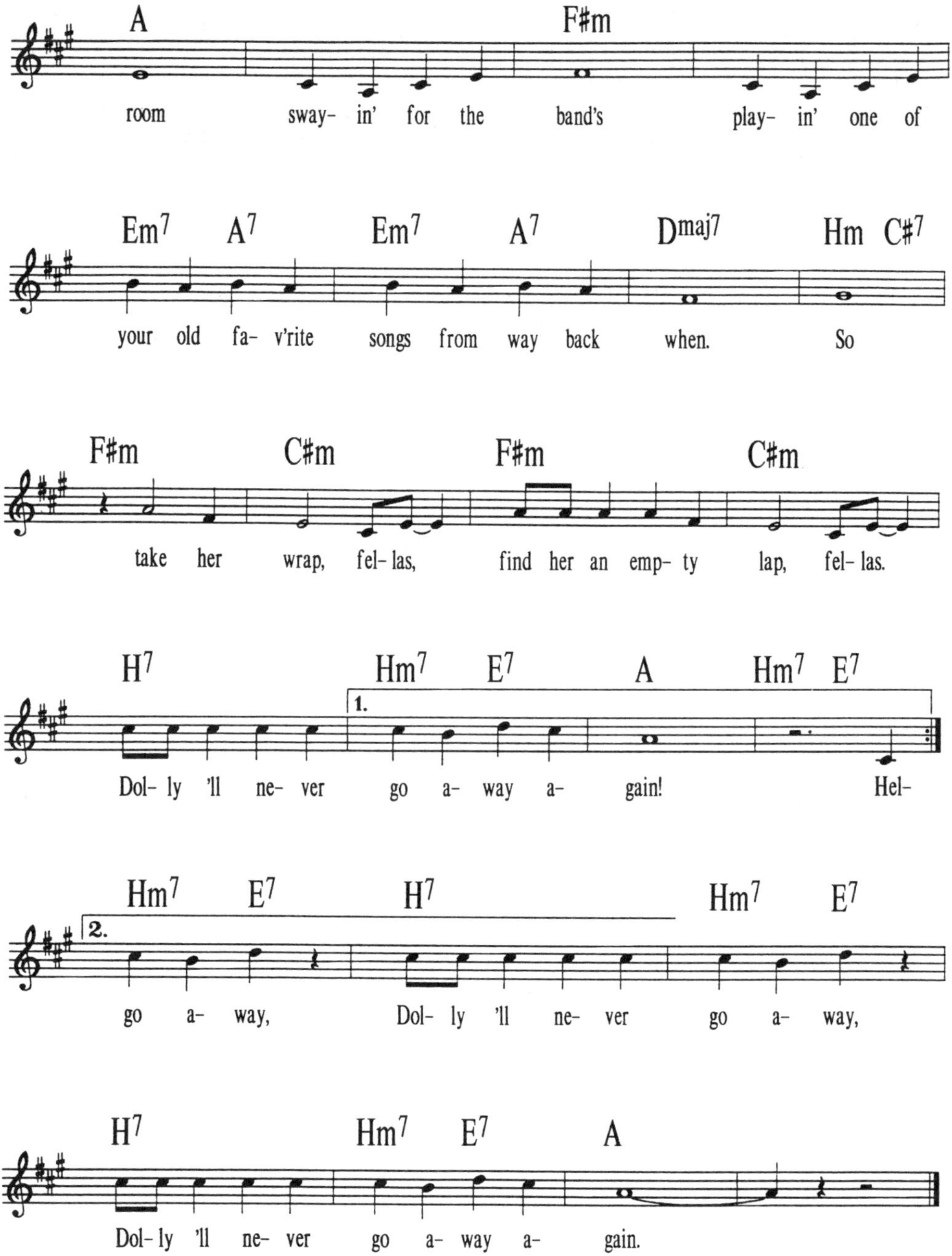
A F#m
room sway- in' for the band's play- in' one of
Em7 A7 Em7 A7 Dmaj7 Hm C#7
your old fa- v'rite songs from way back when. So
F#m C#m F#m C#m
take her wrap, fel- las, find her an emp- ty lap, fel- las.
H7 Hm7 E7 A Hm7 E7
1.
Dol- ly 'll ne- ver go a- way a- gain! Hel-
Hm7 E7 H7 Hm7 E7
2.
go a- way, Dol- ly 'll ne- ver go a- way,
H7 Hm7 E7 A
Dol- ly 'll ne- ver go a- way a- gain.

HERE WE GO LOOBY LOO

Traditional
Rhythmus: Latin
Tempo: Moderato

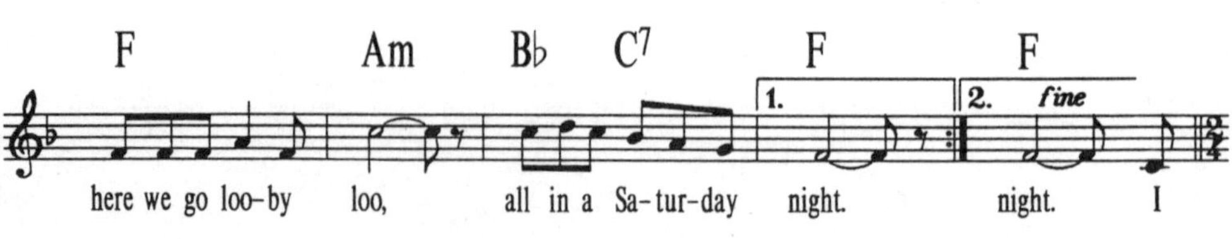

2. Here we go looby loo …
I put my left hand in …

3. Here we go looby loo …
I put my right foot in …

4. Here we go looby loo …
I put my left foot in …

5. Here we go looby loo …
I put my whole self in,
I put my whole self out,
I give myself a shake, shake, shake
And turn myself about. Oh!

ICE CREAM

Musik und Text: Howard Johnson / Billy Moll / Robert King
Rhythmus: Swing
Tempo: Moderato

2. I scream, you scream, we all scream for Ice Cream, Rah! Rah! Rah!
Frosted, malted, or peppered and salted, Siss! Boom! Bah!
Oh! Spumoni, oh, Tortoni, and confidentially, Oh! Oh! Baloney.
I scream, you scream, we all scream for Ice Cream, Rah! Rah! Rah! Rah!

3. Alpha, Beta, a frozen tomaytuh, Yes! Oh! Yes!
Ham and egg a for Lambda Omega, Siss! O. S.
A. B. C. ses, X. Y. Z. ses, But in the winter time no B. V. D. ses.
Ketchup, mustard on fresh cherry cystard Ice Cream Pi. Pi.

IN A GADDA DA VIDA

Musik und Text:
Douglas Ingle
Interpreten: Iron Butterfly
Rhythmus: Rock
Tempo: Moderato

G E7
Oh, won't you come with me
G7 E A
and take my hand? Oh, won't you
F#7 A F# H
come with me and walk this land?
Dm
Please take my hand!

LA JESUCITA

Traditional
Rhythmus: Latin
Tempo: Moderato

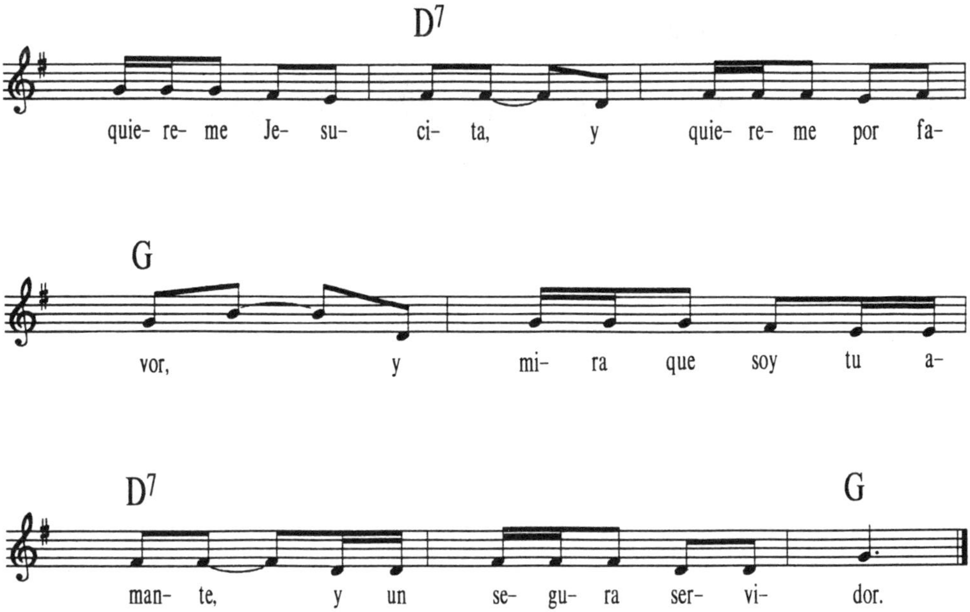

2. Vamos al baile veras que bonito
Donde se alumbran con veinte liternas,
Donde las ninas ensenan las piernas,
Donde se bailan con mucho bacilon.
Y quiereme, Jesucita …

Deutscher Text:

1. Laßt uns zum Tanz gehen, du wirst sehen,
Wie hübsch man es dort
Mit zwanzig Laternen erleuchtet hat.
Wo man die modernen Tänze tanzt,
Wo man mit viel Flirten tanzt.
Und lieb' mich, Jesucita, und lib' mich, bitte,
Und sieh' daß ich dein Liebhaber
Und dein getreuer Diener bin.

2. Laßt uns zum Tanz gehen, du wirst sehen,
Wie hübsch man es dort
Mit zwanzig Laternen erleuchtet hat,
Wo die Mädchen ihre Beine zeigen,
Wo man mit viel Flirten tanzt.
Und lieb mich, Jesucita …

Lola

Musik und Text:
Raymond Douglas Davies
Interpreten: Kinks
Rhythmus: Rock
Tempo: Moderato

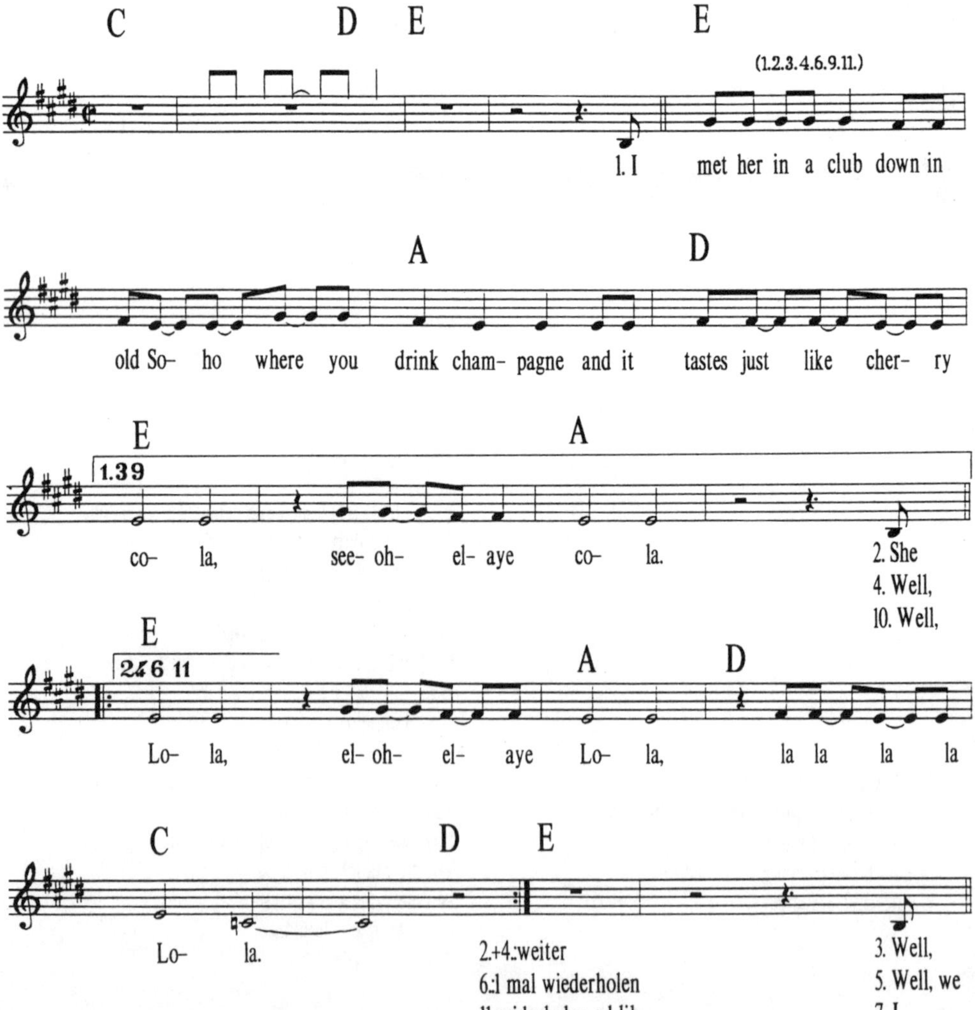

H7 F#
(5.10.)
5. drank cham- pagne and danced all night un- der e- lec- tric can-
A
dle light, she picked me up and sat me on her knee and
said: "Dear boy, won't you come home with me?" 6. Well,
11. Well,
A E H A E H
7. pushed her a- way, I walked to the door,
A E H E G#7 C#m
I fell to the floor, I got down on my knees.
H
Then I looked at her and she at me. 8. Well,
E
that's the way that I want it to stay, and I

2. (A) She walked up to me, and she asked me to dance,
I asked her her name and in a dark brown voice, she said Lola, ...

3. (A) Well, I'm not the world's most physical guy,
But when she squeezed me tight she nearly broke my spine, oh my Lola, ...

4. (A) Well, I'm not dumb, but I can't understand
Why she walked like a woman and a talked like a man, oh my Lola, ...

6. (A) Well, I'm not the world's most passionate guy,
But when I looked in her eyes, well, I almost fell for my Lola, ...

9. (A) Girls will be boys and boys will be girls,
It's a mixed up, muddled up, shook up world except for Lola, ...

10. (B) Well, I left home just a week before and I'd never ever kissed a woman before.
But Lola smiled and took me by the hand and said "Dear boy, I'm gonna make you a man."

11. (A) Well, I'm not the world's most masculine man,
But I know what I am, and I'm glad I'm a man and so is Lola, ...

London Street

Traditional
Rhythmus: Medium Song
Tempo: Moderato

2. I shook my foot on London Street,
London Street, London Street.
I shook my foot on London Street
On a cold, frosty morning.

3. I shook my head on London Street,
London Street, London Street.
I shook my head on London Street
On a cold, frosty morning.

LOVE IS IN THE AIR

Musik und Text:
Harry Vanda / George Young
Rhythmus: Latin
Tempo: Moderato

2. Love is in the air in the rising of the sun, love is in the air when the day is nearly done.
And I don't know if you're illusion, don't know if I see it true.
But you're something that I must believe in, and you're there when I reach out for you.
Love is in the air, ev'ry sight and ev'ry sound. And I don't know if I'm being foolish,
Don't know if I'm being wise, but it's something that I must believe in, and it's there when I look in your eyes.

Melodie in F

Musik: Anton Rubinstein
Classical
Tempo: Moderato

Gm C7 F
C Cdim G G7 C
Cdim G G7 C
Fm C Fm C
Fm C Fm C Fm C
D.C. al fine

Memphis, Tennessee

Interpret: Chuck Berry
Rhythmus: Rock
Tempo: Moderato

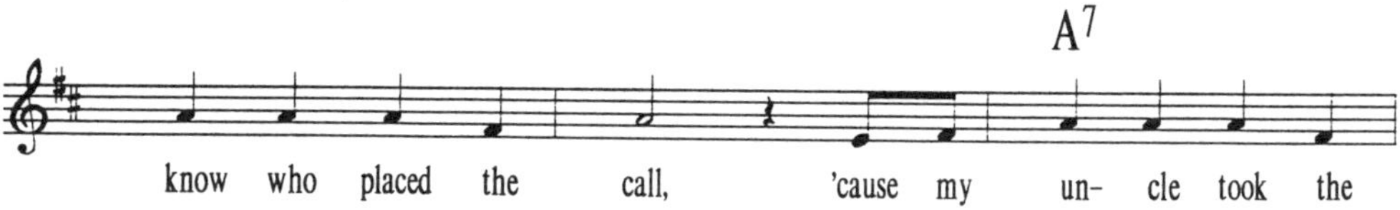

2. Help me, information, get in touch with my Marie.
She's the only one who'd phone me here from Memphis, Tennessee.
Her home is on the south side, high up on a ridge,
Just a half a mile from the Mississippi Bridge.

3. Help me, information, more than I cannot add.
Only that I miss her and all the fun we had.
But we were pulled apart, because her mom did not agree,
And tore apart our happy home in Memphis, Tennessee.

4. Last time I saw Marie, she's waving me goodbye,
With hurry home drops on her cheek that trickled from her eye.
Marie is only six years old, information, please,
And try to put me through to her in Memphis, Tennessee.

muß i denn ...

Traditional
Interpret: Elvis Presley
Rhythmus: Medium Rock
Tempo: Moderato

2. Wie du weinst, wie du weinst,
Daß i wandere muß,
Wie wenn d'Lieb jetzt wär vorbei.
Sind au drauß, sind au drauß
Der Mädele viel,
Lieber Schatz, i bleib dir treu.
Denk du net, wenn i ein' andre seh,
No sei mein' Lieb vorbei.
Sind au drauß, sind au drauß
Der Mädele viel,
Lieber Schatz, i bleib dir treu.

3. Übers Jahr, übers Jahr,
Wenn mer träubele schneid't,
Stell i hier mi wiedrum ein.
Bin i dann, bin i dann
Dein Schätzele noch,
So soll die Hochzeit sein.
Übers Jahr, do ist mein Zeit vorbei,
Do g'hör i mein und dein.
Bin i dann, bin i dann
Dein Schätzele noch,
so soll die Hochzeit sein.

My Sweet Lord

Musik und Text:
George Harrison
Interpret: George Harrison
Rhythmus: Medium Rock
Tempo: Moderate

D Am D Am
My sweet Lord, um, my Lord,
D Am D
um, my Lord. I real- ly want to
G G7 E7
see you. Real-ly want to see you. Real-ly want to see you Lord.
A E° Hm
Real-ly want to see you Lord. But it takes so long my Lord.
E Hm E Hm E
fade out
My sweet Lord, um, my Lord, my sweet Lord

MY WAY

Musik: Claude Francois / Jaques Revaux
Originaltext: Gilles Thibaut
Englischer Text: Paul Anka
Interpreten: Paul Anka, Elvis Presley, Frank Sinatra
Rhythmus: Slow Rock

D/A A7 Em/D D
1.
more, much more than this I did it my way. Re–
D Am/D
2.
way. Yes, there were times, I'm sure you know, when I bit
G Em7
off more than I could chew. But through it all when there was
A7 F#m Hm Em7
doubt I ate it up and spit it out, I faced it all and I stood
A Em/D D D
D.S.
tall and did it my way. 2. I've way.

Nobody Knows The Troubles I've Seen

Traditional
Interpret: Mahalia Jackson
Rhythmus: Medium Song
Tempo: Moderato

2. Now, you may think that I don't know,
Nobody knows but Jesus.
But I've had my troubles here below,
Glory Hallelujah!

3. One day when I was walkin' along,
Nobody knows but Jesus.
The sky opened up and love came down,
Glory Hallelujah!

4. What make old Satan hate me so?
Nobody knows but Jesus.
He had me once and had to let me go,
Glory Hallelujah!

5. I never shall forget that day,
Nobody knows but Jesus.
When Jesus washed my sins away,
Glory Hallelujah!

Only One Woman

Musik und Text:
Barry Gibb / Robin Gibb / Maurice Gibb
Interpreten: Bee Gees, Alien, Ochsenknecht
Rhythmus: Ballade
Tempo: Medium

2. Who sees my lonely face? Who sees my shame?
Nobody in the place can tell me her name,
`Cause she was only one woman …

3. Ten little indians, now there are none,
I bet there are many and her love still goes on,
`Cause she was only one woman …

Out Of Time

Musik und Text:
Mick Jagger / Keith Richard
Interpreten: Rolling Stones, Chris Farlowe
Rhythmus: Rock
Tempo: Moderato

2. A girl who wants to run away, discovers that she's had her day.
It's no good you thinking that you are still mine,
You're out of touch my baby, my poor unfaithful baby,
I said baby, baby, baby, you're out of time.

3. You thought you were a clever girl, giving up your social whirl
But you can't come back and be the first in line,
You're absolute my baby, my poor old fashioned baby,
I said baby, baby, baby, you're out of time.

Oye Como Va

Musik und Text:
Tito Puente
Interpreten: Santana
Rhythmus: Latin Rock
Tempo: Moderato

Am7 D Am7
D Am D Am
f
mf
Am7 D Am7 D
3
Am7 D Am7
D Am7 D
Am7 D Am7
D Am7 D
Am D Am
ff

PAINT IT BLACK

Musik und Text:
Mick Jagger / Keith Richard
Interpreten: Rolling Stones
Rhythmus: Rock
Tempo: Moderato

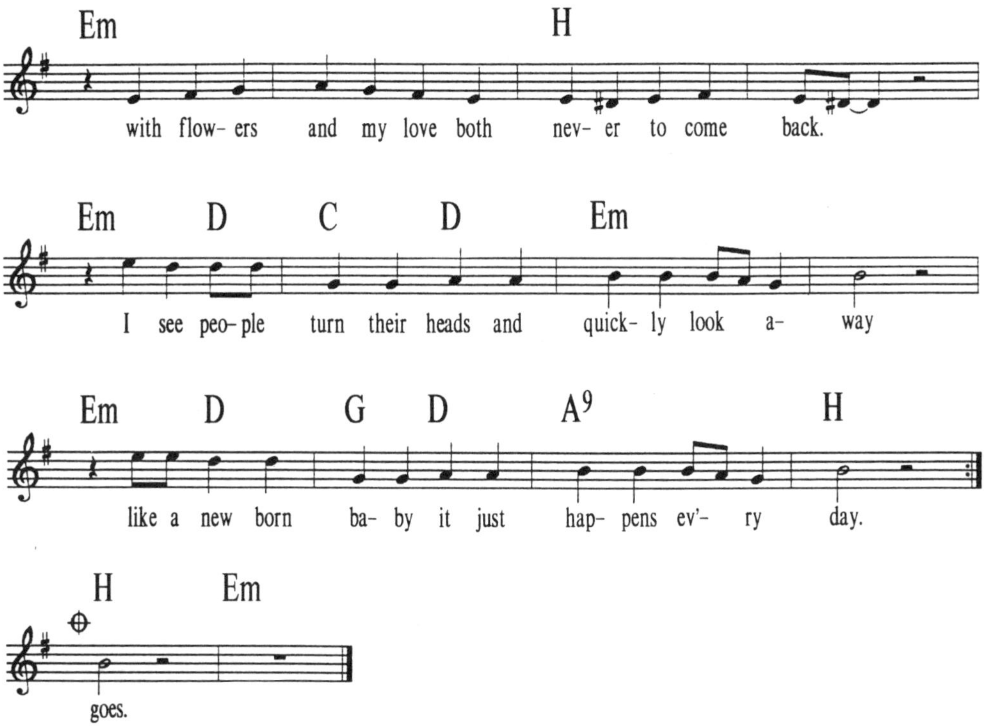

3. I look inside myself and see my heart is black.
I see my red door and I want it painted black.
Maybe then I'll fade away and not have to face the facts,
It's not easy facing up when your whole world is black.

4. No more will my green sea go turn a deeper blue,
I could not fore see this thing happening to you.
If I look hard enough into the setting sun,
My love will laugh with me before the morning comes.

Paloma Blanca

Musik und Text:
Hans Bouwens
Interpreten: George Baker Selection
Rhythmus: Pop
Tempo: Moderato

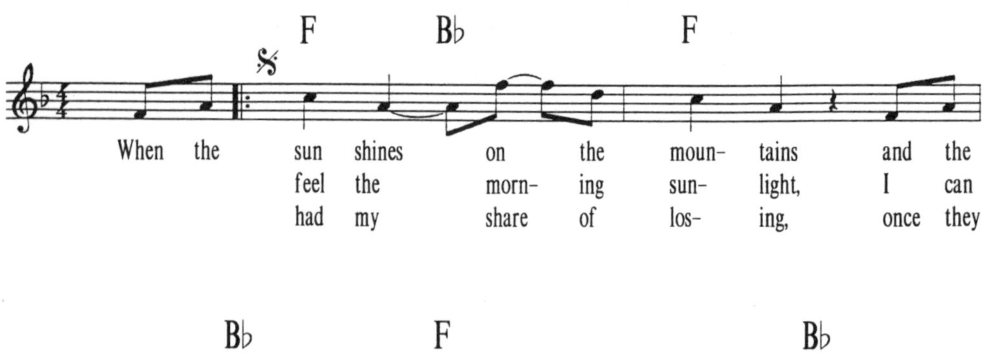

2. 3
F
B♭
U- na Pa- lo- ma Blan- ca,
F
B♭
I'm just a bird in the sky. U- na Pa- lo- ma Blan- ca,
F
C
o- ver the moun- tains I fly. No one can take
F
fine
D.S.
my free- dom a- way. Once I

Please, Mr. Postman

Musik: Georgia Dobbins /
William Garrett / Brian Holland
Text: Robert Bateman / Freddie Goreman
Interpreten: Beatles
Rhythmus: Medium Rock
Tempo: Moderato

B♭
You did- n't stop to make me feel bet- ter
F
1.
Folge
if there's a let- ter, a let- ter for me.
2.
D.S. al ⊕ ⊕
E♭
card or a let- ter, Mis-ter I've been stand-ing here wait-ing Mis-ter Post- man,
Gm
E♭
so pa- tient- ly for just a card
F
or just a let- ter say-ing he's re-turn-ing home to me. Mis- ter
⊕
F
N.C.
such a long time. Why don't you check it and see one more
B♭
time for me. You got- ta wait a min- ute, wait a min- ute,
Gm
E♭
wait a min-ute, wait a min-ute, ooo Mis- ter Post- Mis- ter Post- man
F
N.C.
Repeat and fade
man. Come on de- liv- er the let- ter; the soon- er the bet- ter.

WALK ON THE WILD SIDE

Musik und Text:
Lou Reed
Interpret: Lou Reed
Rhythmus: Rock
Tempo: Moderato

2. Candy came from out on the island,in the backroom she was ev'rybody's darling,
But she never lost her head, even when she was given head she said, hey babe, take a walk on the wild side s...

3. Little Joe never once gave it away, ev'rybody had to pay and pay.
A hustle here and a hustle there, New York city is ni place where they said, hey babe, take a walk on the wild side...

4. Sugar plum fairy came and hit the streets, looking for soul food and a place to eat,
went to the Apollo, you should have seen him go go go, they said, hey sugar, take a walk on the wild side...

5. Jackie is just speeding away, thought she was James Dean for a day,
Then I guess she had to crash, valium would have helped that bash, she said, hey sugar, take a walk on the wild side...

We Are Family

Musik und Text:
Bernard Edwards / Nile Rodgers
Interpreten: Sister Sledge
Rhythmus: Disco Rock
Tempo: Moderato

G D F/G A7
We are fa- mi- ly. I got all my sis- ters with me.
G D F/G
We are fa- mi- ly. Get up ev'- ry- bo- dy and sing.
A Em7 D9 A Em7
Liv-ing life is fun, and we've just be- gun to get our share of this worlds
D9 A Em7 D9 A Em7
de- lights. High hopes we have for the fu- ture. And our
D9 A Em7 D9
goal's in sight. No, we don't get de- pressed. Here's what we call
A Em7 D9 A Em7
our gol- den rule: Have faith in you and the
D9 A Em7 D9 A7
things you do. You won't go wrong. This is our fam- 'ly jew- el.
A7 G D F/G A7
We are fa- mi- ly. I got all my sis- ters with me.
G D F/G A7
repeat and fade
We are fa- mi- ly. Get up, ev'- ry- bo- dy, and sing.

Rock & Roll Music

Musik und Text:
Chuck Berry
Interpreten: Chuck Berry, Beatles
Rhythmus: Rock 'n' Roll
Tempo: Moderao

C
Mu- sic. If you wan- na dance with me.
G7 C
If you wan- na dance with me. I've got no kick a- gainst
Don't care to hear 'em play
G7 C
mo- dern jazz. Un- less they try to play it too dam fast,
a tan- go. I'm in the mood to dig a mam- bo,
F
And change the beau- ty of the me- lo- dy. Un- til they sound- ed like a
it's 'way too ear- ly for a con- go. So keep a- rock- in' that pi-
G7
second time: D.S. al fine
Fine
sym- pho- ny. That's why I go for that
a- no. So I can hear some of that

Sacrifice

Musik und Text:
Elton John / Bernie Taupin
Interpret: Elton John
Rhythmus: Ballade
Tempo: Moderato

E A D
when the cent of her lin- gers and temp- ta- tion's strong
sen- si- ti- vi- ty builds a prison in the fi- nal act.
Hm7 E Fm
in- to the boun- dary
We lose di- rec- tion.
D E
of each mar- ried hand. Sweet de- ceit comes a call
no stone up turned, no tears to damn
F#m D E
in' and ne- ga- ti- vi- ty lands. Cold, cold heart.
you when jea-lou-sy burns.
A D Hm7 E
hard done by you. Some things look bet- ter,

A D E
ba- by, just pas- sing through.
A D
And it's no sa- cri- fice, just a sim- ple word.
E
It's two hearts liv- ing in two sep- ar- ate worlds.
A
But it's no sa- cri- fice, no sa-
Hm C#m7
cri- fice, it's no sa- cri- fice

D E7 A C#m7 Dadd9
1.
at all.
2. Mu-tual mis- un- der-stand-
2.
A D
C#m7 E A
D C#m7 E
D.S.
Cold, cold heart,
A D C#m7 E
repeat and fade
No sa- cri- fice at all.

SAIL ALONG SILV'RY MOON

Musik und Text:
Percy Wenrich / Harry Tobias
Rhythmus: Slow Rock
Tempo: Slow

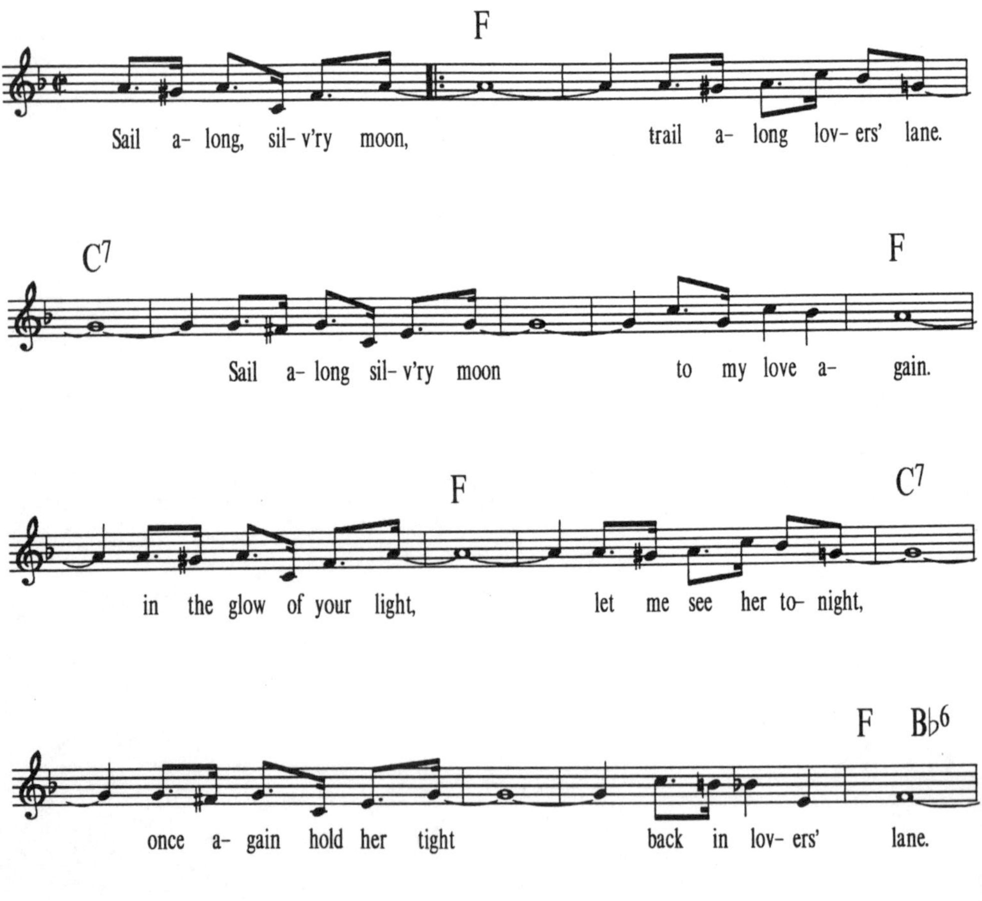

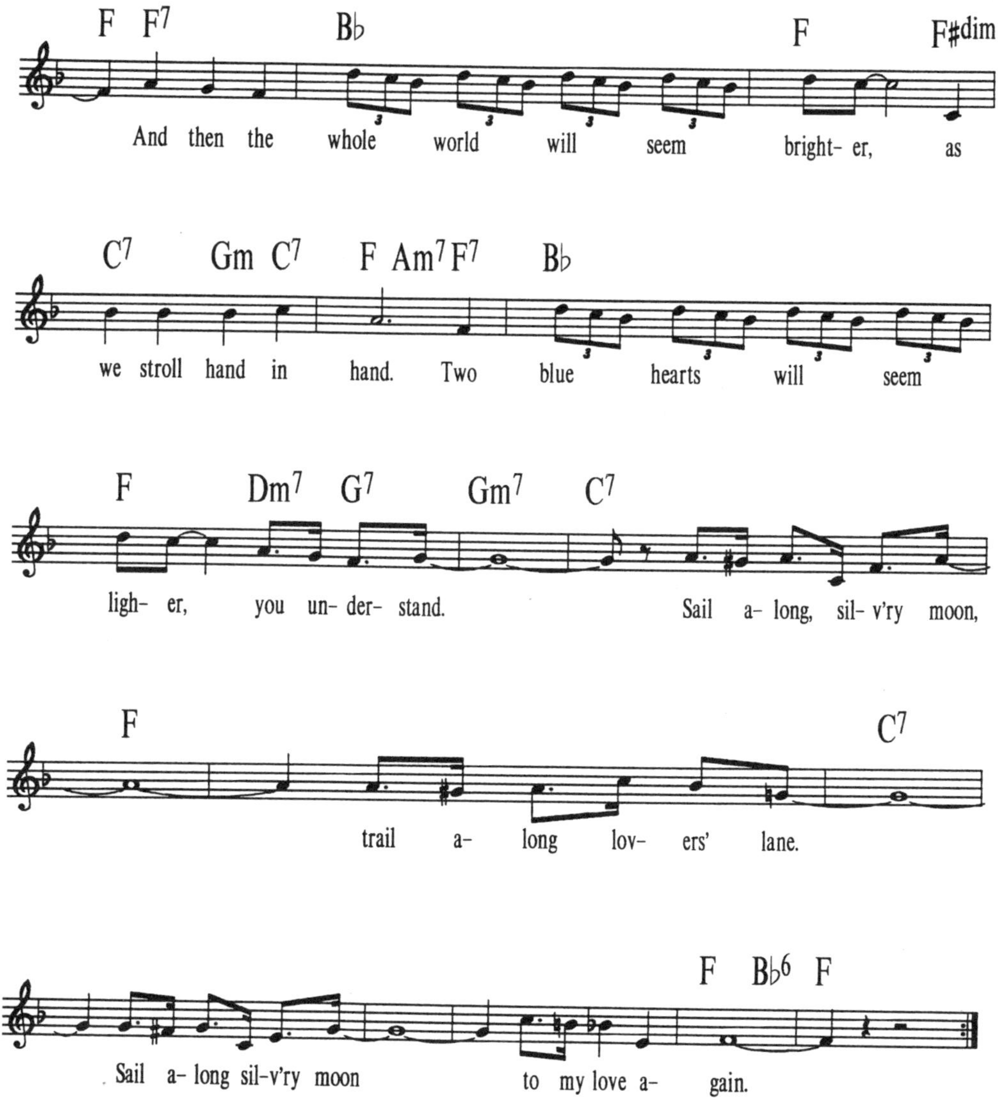
F F7 B♭ F F♯dim
And then the whole world will seem bright- er, as
C7 Gm C7 F Am7 F7 B♭
we stroll hand in hand. Two blue hearts will seem
F Dm7 G7 Gm7 C7
ligh- er, you un- der- stand. Sail a- long, sil- v'ry moon,
F C7
trail a- long lov- ers' lane.
F B♭6 F
Sail a- long sil- v'ry moon to my love a- gain.

SKIP TO MY LOU

Traditional
Rhythmus: Medium Song
Tempo: Moderato

2. Flies in the buttermilk, shoo fly, shoo!
Flies in the buttermilk, shoo fly, shoo!
Flies in the buttermilk, shoo fly, shoo!
Skip to my Lou, my darling.

3. Lost my partner, what`ll I do?
Lost my partner, what`ll I do?
Lost my partner, what`ll I do?
Skip to my Lou, my darling.

4. Find you another, prettier too.
Find you another, prettier too.
Find you another, prettier too.
Skip to my Lou, my darling.

Something's Gotten Hold of My Heart

Musik und Text:
Roger Cook / Roger Greenaway
Interpret: Gene Pitney
Rhythmus: Ballade
Tempo: Moderato

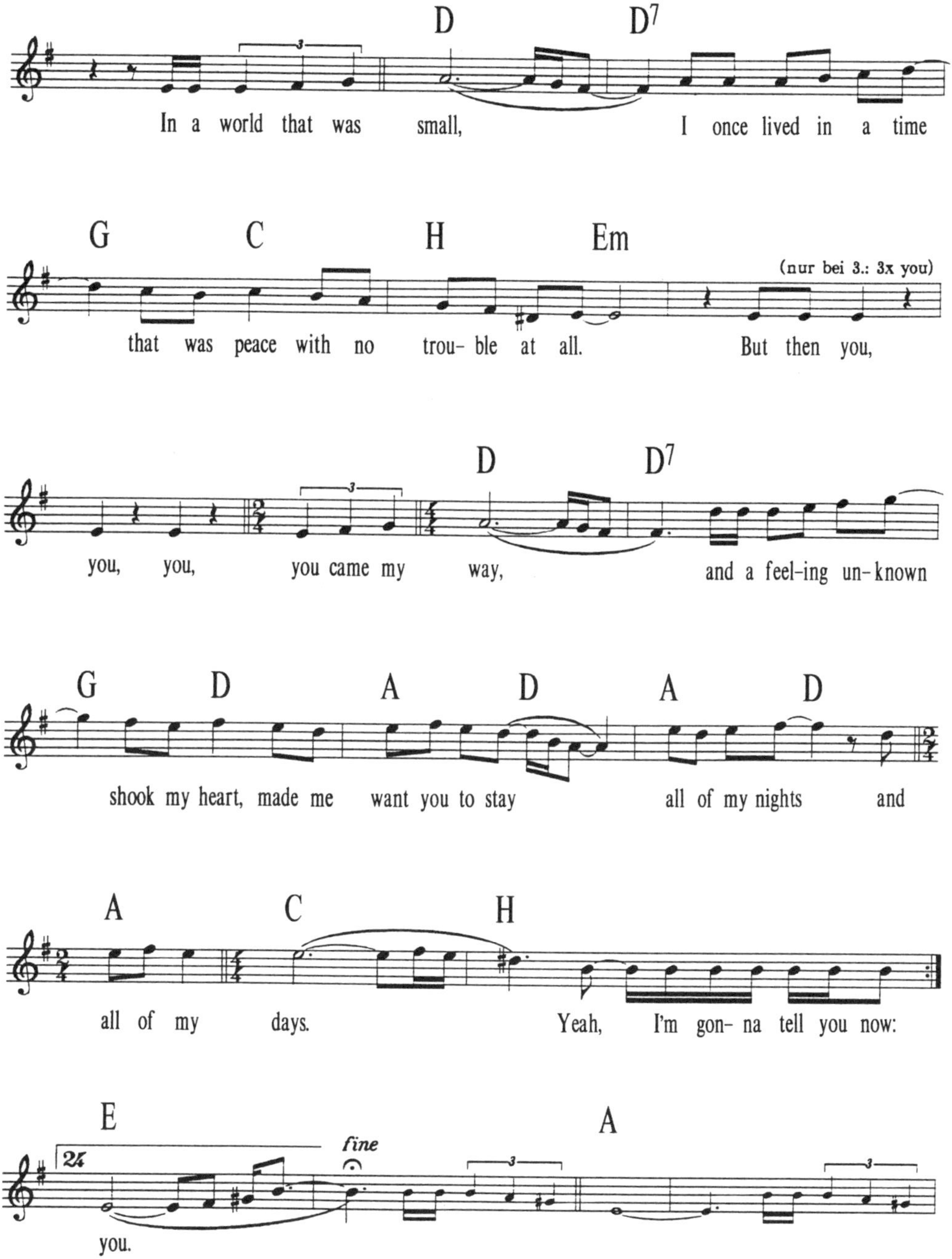
D D7
In a world that was small, I once lived in a time
G C H Em
(nur bei 3.: 3x you)
that was peace with no trou- ble at all. But then you,
D D7
you, you, you came my way, and a feel-ing un-known
G D A D A D
shook my heart, made me want you to stay all of my nights and
A C H
all of my days. Yeah, I'm gon- na tell you now:
E A
2x
fine
you.

E A F#
I've
F#7
got to know if this is the real thing,
I've got to know what's mak-ing my heart sing, wo oh oh,
H H7
yeah, you smile and I am lost for a life-
H9
time, each min- ute spend with you is the right time, ev'- ry hour
H7
yeah, ev'- ry day yeah, you

2. Something's gotten hold of my hand dragging my soul to a beautiful land.
Yeah, something has invaded my night painting my sleep with a colour so bright.
Changing the grey, changing the blue, scarlet for me and scarlet for you.

3. Something's gotten hold of my hand dragging my soul to a beautiful land.
Something's gotten into my life cutting it's way through my dreams like a knife.
Turning me up, turning me down, making me smile, making me frown.

4. Something's gotten hold of my heart keeping my soul and my senses apart.
Yeah, something's has invaded my night painting my sleep with a colour so bright.
Changing the grey, changing the blue, scarlet for me and scarlet for you.

Yes Sir, That's My Baby

Musik: Walter Donaldson
Text: Gus Kahn
Rhythmus: Charleston
Tempo: Moderato

2. Well, well, "look-it" that baby,
Do tell, don't say "may-be" Nell's Bells,
Won't she cause some row. Pretty soon, pretty soon
We will hear that Lohengrin tune,
Who for should she be, Sir? No one else but me, Sir.

St. Louis *Blues*

Musik und Text:
W. C. Handy
Rhythmus: Swing
Tempo: Moderato

2. Feelin' tomorrow lak ah feel today.
Feelin' tomorrow lak ah feel today.
I'll pack my trunk make ma git away.

3. Been to the gipsy to get ma fortune tole.
Been to the gipsy to get ma fortune tole.
`Cause I'm is wile 'baut ma Jelly Roll.

4. Gipsy done tole me "Don't you wear no black"
Yas she done tole me "Don't you wear no black"
Go to St. Louis you can win him back.

5. Blacker than midnight theet lak flags o'truce.
Blackest man in the whole St. Louis.
Blacker de berry sweeter are the juice.

Sur Le Pont D'Avignon

Traditional aus Frankreich
Rhythmus: Medium Song
Tempo: Moderato

TAKE ME HOME COUNTRY ROADS

Musik und Text:
Bill Danoff / John Denver / Taffy Nivert
Interpret: John Denver
Rhythmus: Country
Tempo: Moderato

E D
mom- ma, take me home, Coun- try
A F#m
1. 2.
Roads. All my I hear her
E A D
voice, in the mor- nin' hour she calls me, the ra- di- o re-
A E F#m
minds me of my home far a- way, and driv- in' down the
G D A
road I get a feel- in' that I should have been home-
E E7
D.S.
yes- ter- day, yes- ter- day. Coun- try
A E
Roads, take me home, Coun- try
A E A
Roads, take me home, Coun- try Roads.

THE DOCK OF THE BAY

Musik und Text:
Steve Cropper / Otis Redding
Interpret: Otis Redding
Rhythmus: Soul
Tempo: Slow

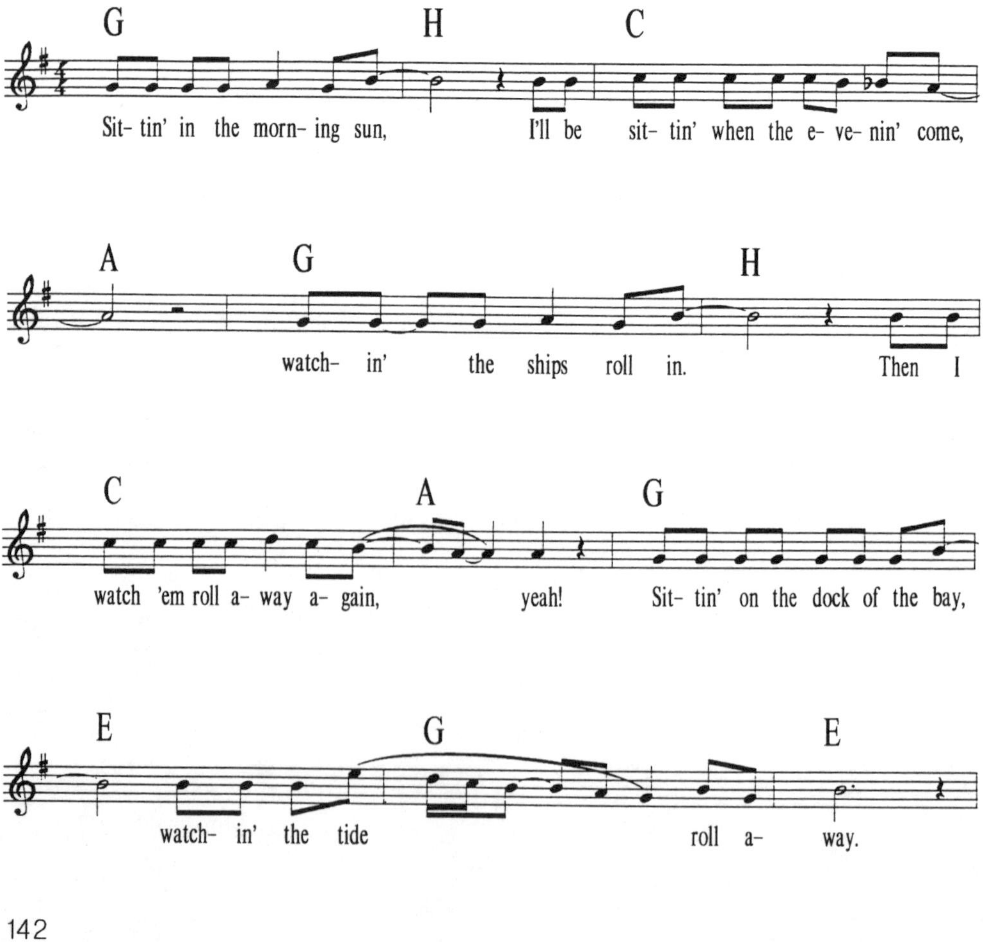

2. I left my home in Georgia, headed for the Frisco Bay.
I have nothing to live for, look like nothing gonna come my way.
So I'm just gonna sit on the dock of the bay, watchin' the tide roll away.
Sittin' on the dock of the bay, wastin' time.

THE DRUNKEN SAILOR

Traditional
Rhythmus: Shanty
Tempo: Allegro

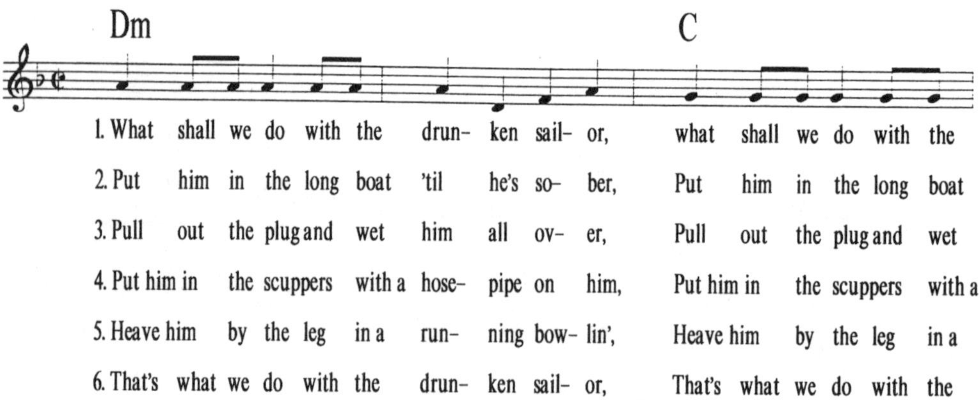

1. Ho, unser Maat, ja der hat schief geladen,
Ho, unser Maat, ja der hat schief geladen,
Ho, unser Maat, ja der hat schief geladen,
Morgens in der Frühe.
Hoio, ahoi! Wir segeln,
Hoio, ahoi, wir segeln,
Hoio, ahoi! Wir segeln morgens in der Frühe.

2. Wie bringen wir ihn wieder auf die Beine,
Wie bringen wir ihn wieder auf die Beine,
Wie bringen wir ihn wieder auf die Beine,
Morgens in der Frühe?
Hoio, ahoi! Wir segeln,
Hoio, ahoi, wir segeln,
Hoio, ahoi! Wir segeln morgens in der Frühe.

3. Gebt ihm doch einen Eimer kaltes Wasser,
Gebt ihm doch einen Eimer kaltes Wasser,
Gebt ihm doch einen Eimer kaltes Wasser,
Morgens in der Frühe.
Hoio, ahoi! Wir segeln,
Hoio, ahoi, wir segeln,
Hoio, ahoi! Wir segeln morgens in der Frühe.

4. Klatsch! Dieser Guß, der macht ihn wieder munter.
Klatsch! Dieser Guß, der macht ihn wieder munter.
Klatsch! Dieser Guß, der macht ihn wieder munter.
Morgens in der Frühe.
Hoio, ahoi! Wir segeln,
Hoio, ahoi, wir segeln,
Hoio, ahoi! Wir segeln morgens in der Frühe.

THE HIPPY HIPPY SHAKE

Musik und Text:
C. Romera
Rhythmus: Rock
Tempo: Moderato

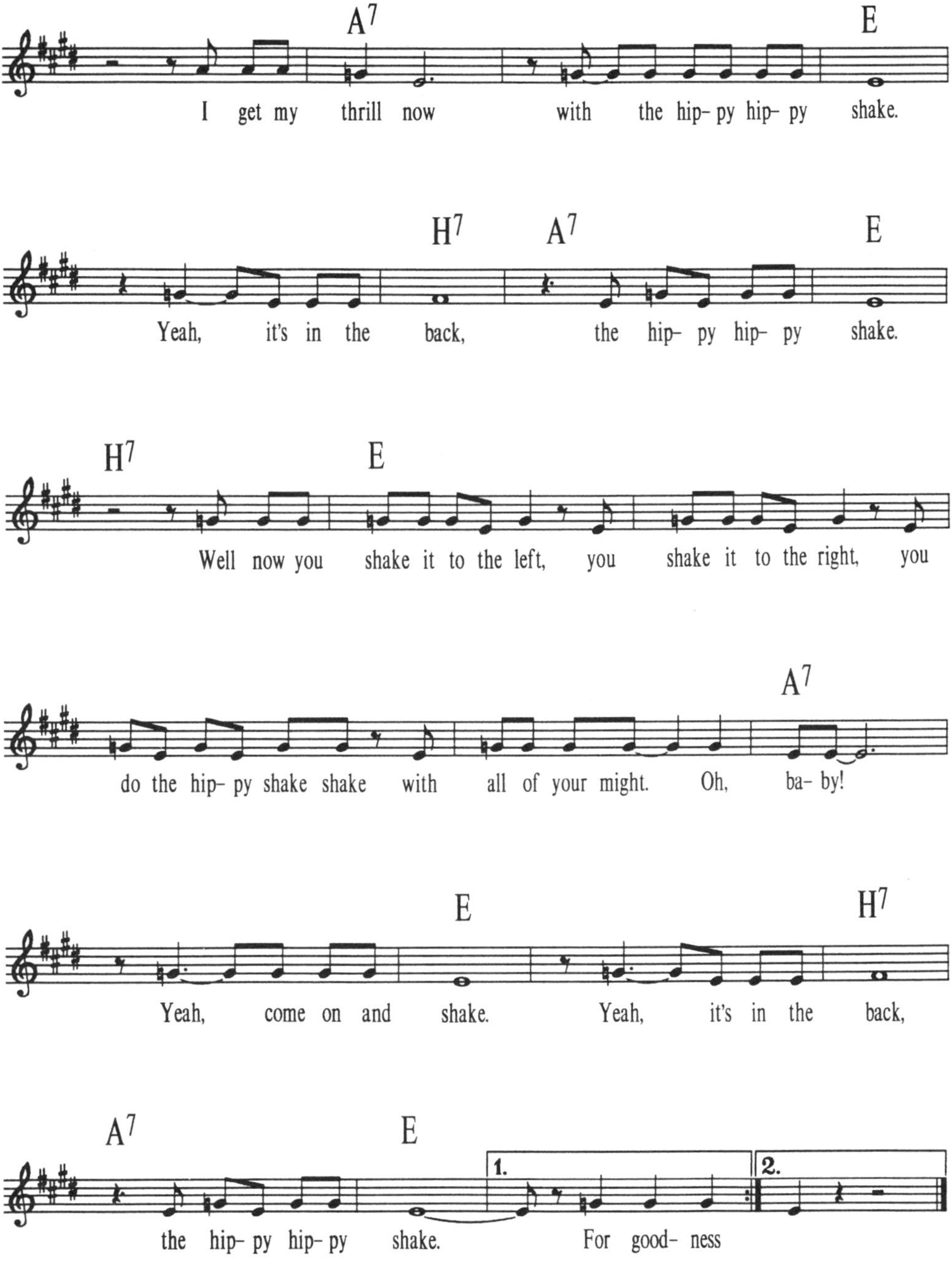
A7
E
I get my thrill now with the hip- py hip- py shake.
H7
A7
E
Yeah, it's in the back, the hip- py hip- py shake.
H7
E
Well now you shake it to the left, you shake it to the right, you
A7
do the hip- py shake shake with all of your might. Oh, ba- by!
E
H7
Yeah, come on and shake. Yeah, it's in the back,
A7
E
1.
2.
the hip- py hip- py shake. For good- ness

THE LAST TIME

Musik und Text:
Mick Jagger / Keith Richard
Interpreten: Rolling Stones
Rhythmus: Rock
Tempo: Moderato

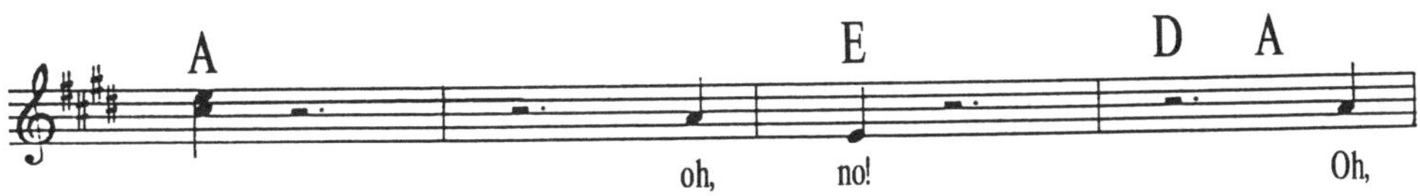

2. Well, I'm sorry girl, but I can't stay
Feeling like I do today,
It's too much pain and too much sorrow,
Guess I'll feel the same tomorrow.
Well this could be the last time ...

3. Well, I told you once and I told you twice
That someone will have to pay the price,
But here's a chance to change your mind
`Cuz I'll be gone a long, long time.
Well this could be the last time ...

The Letter

Musik und Text:
Wayne Carson
Interpreten: Box Tops, Joe Cocker
Rhythmus: Rock
Tempo: Moderato

E7 Am
ba- by just wrote me a let- ter. Well she
C G F C G
wrote me a let- ter said she could- n't live with- out me no more.
C G F C G
List-en mis- ter can't you see I got to get back to my ba- by once more,
E7 Am F
an- y way. Give me a tick- et for an air- plane,
Am7 D7 Am
ain't got time to take the fast- est train. Lone- ly days are gone,
F7 E7 Am
1.
I'm a- go-in' home, my ba- by just wrote me a let- ter. Well she
Am E7 Am
2.
let- ter. My ba- by just wrote me a let- ter. My

There's A Kind Of Hush

Musik und Text:
Les Reed / Geoll Stephens
Interpreten: The Carpenters, Herman's Hermits
Rhythmus: Rock
Tempo: Moderato

F7+ F6 C
clo- ser now and you will see what I mean,
C7 F
it is- n't a dream. The on- ly sound that
F6 F7+ F6 G7
you will hear is when I whis- per in your ear: I love you
C
for ev-er and ev- er. There's a kind of hush
E7 Am C7
all ov- er the world to- night, all ov- er the world
F G7 C G7
(diese 2 Takte am Ende: 4 mal und Fine)
D.S.
you can hear the sounds of lov-ers in love. 3. La la
3. peo- ple just like us are fal- ling in love.
fine

Tinga Layo

Traditional
Rhythmus: Latin
Tempo: Moderato

G D A7 D
walk, my don- key talk, my don- key eat with a knife and fork. Tin- ga
G D A7 D
La- yo, come lit- tle don- key, come, Tin- ga
G D A7 D
La- yo, come lit- tle don- key, come.

Dur | **Moll** | **Dur7** | **Moll7**

C
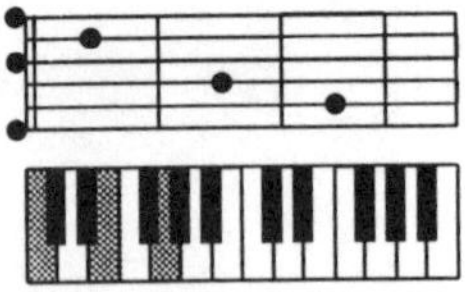
Cm
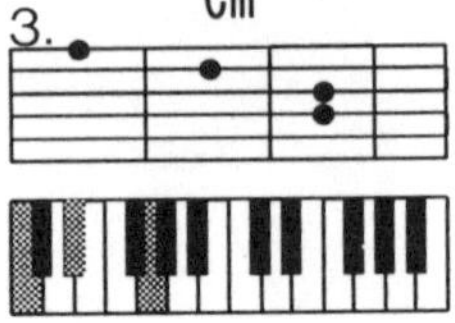
C7
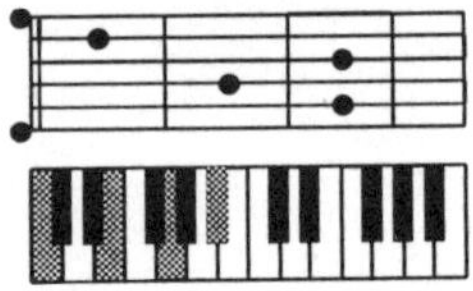
Cm7
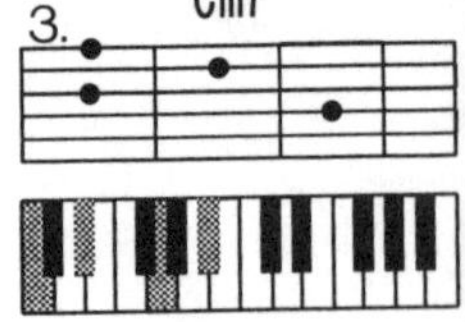

C# / D♭
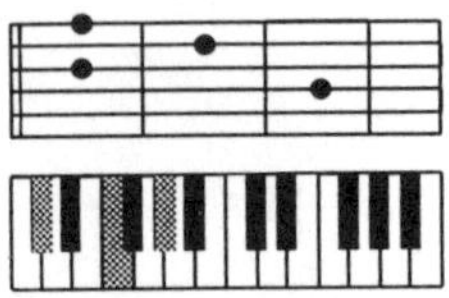
C#m / D♭m
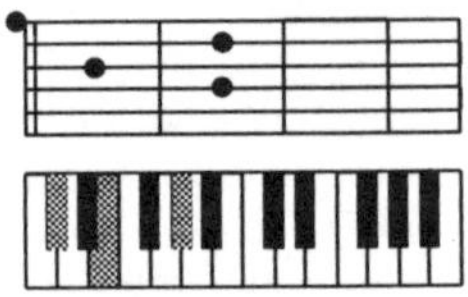
C#7 / D♭7
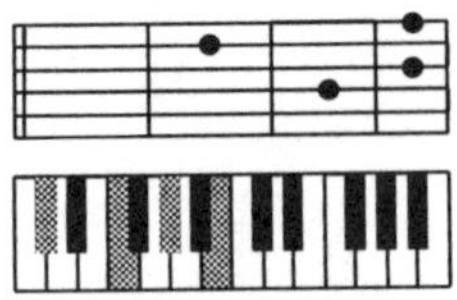
C#m7 / D♭m7
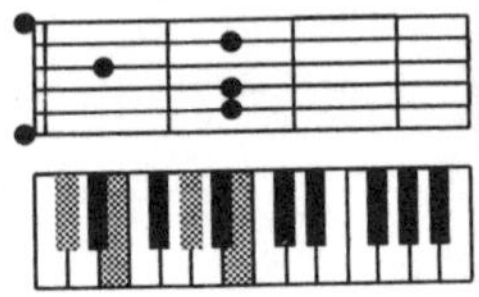

D
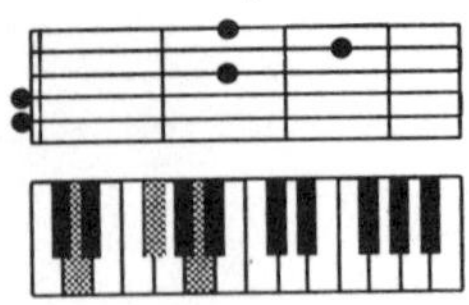
Dm
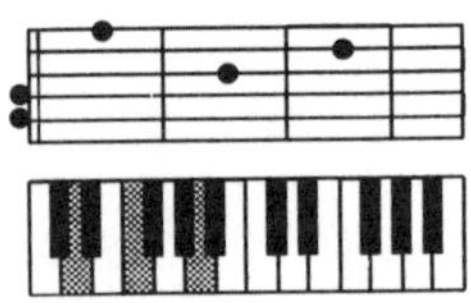
D7
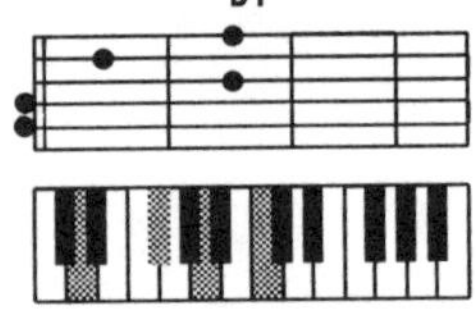
Dm7
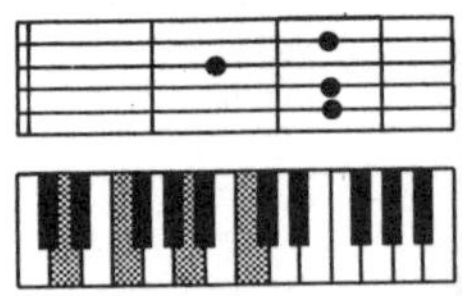

D# / E♭
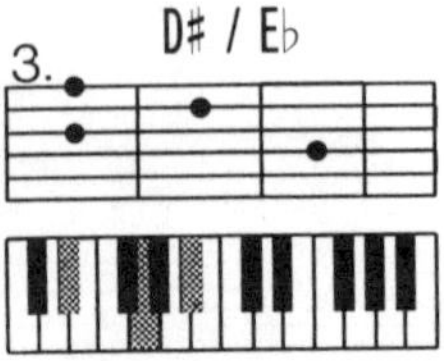
D#m / E♭m
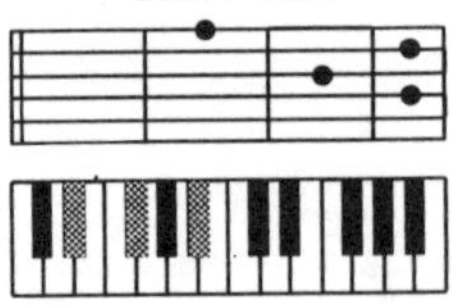
D#7 / E♭7
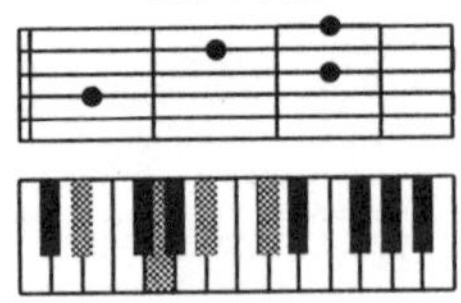
D#m7 / E♭m7
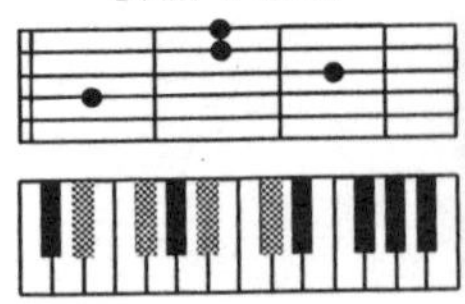

E
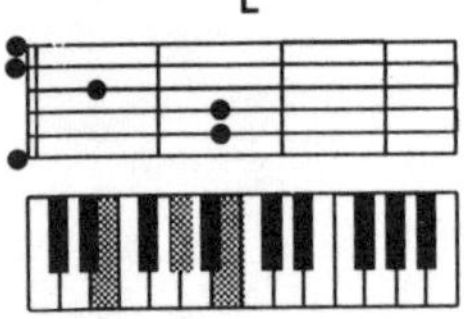
Em
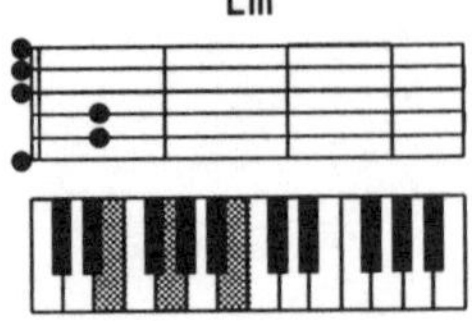
E7
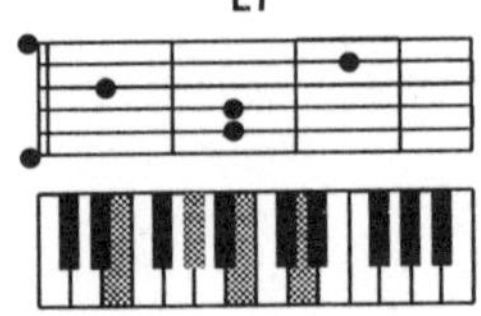
Em7
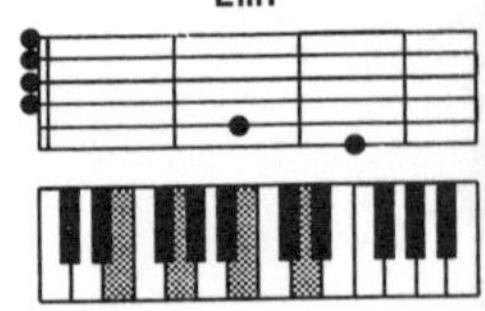

F
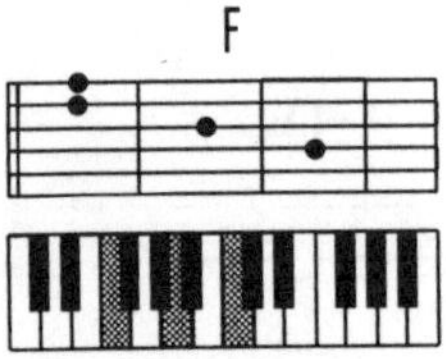
Fm
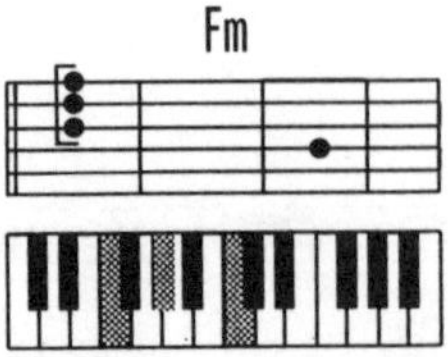
F7
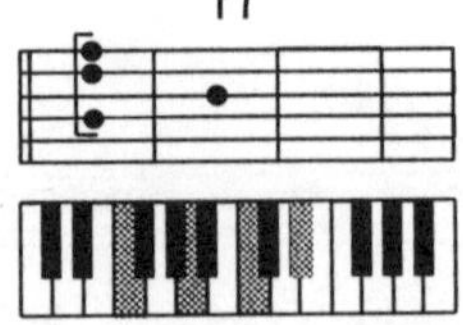
Fm7
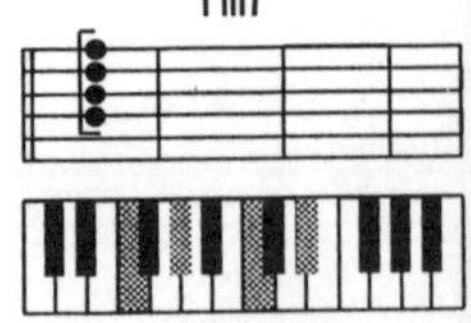

Dur | Moll | Dur7 | Moll7

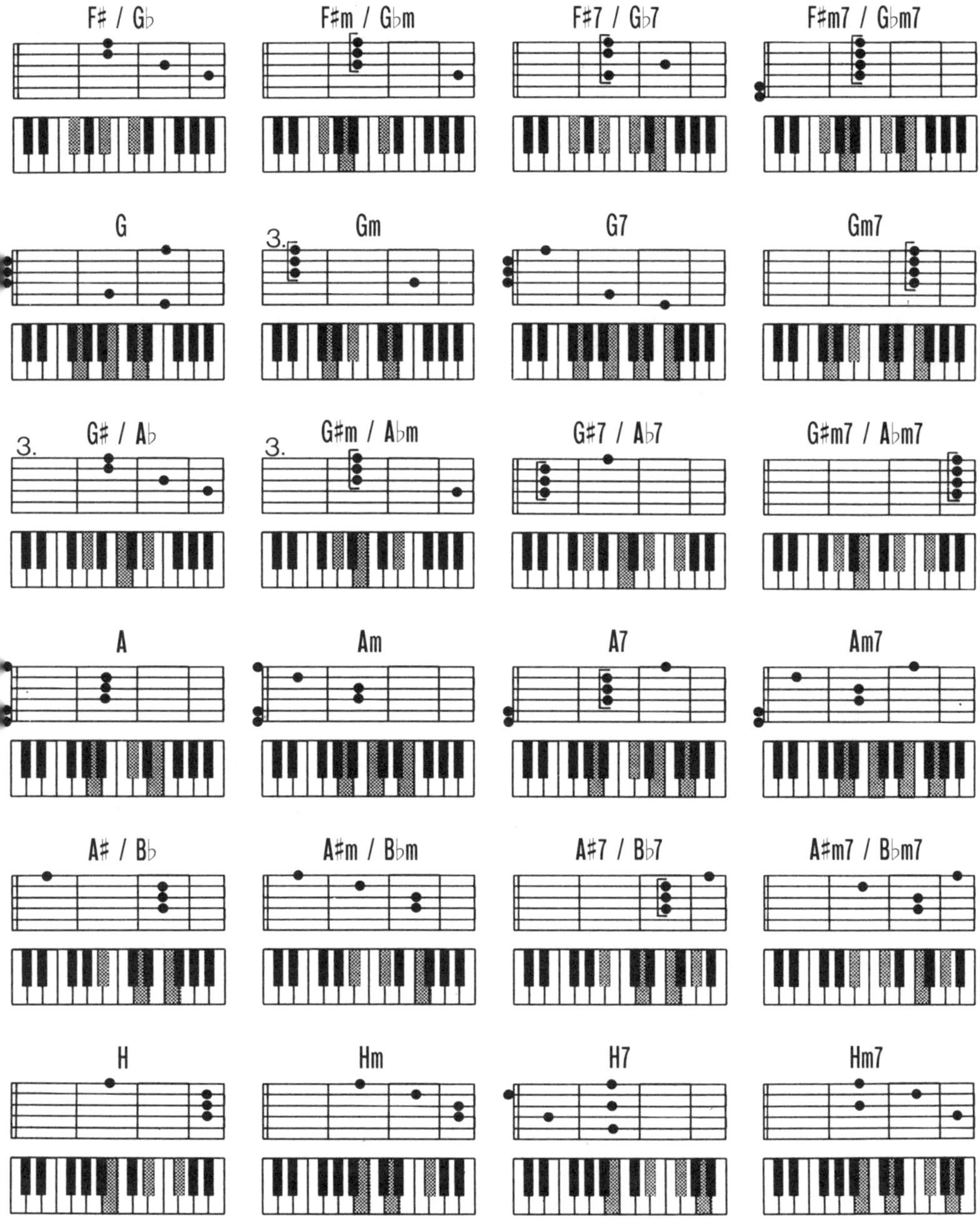

Dur^{maj7} Dur^{sus4} o +

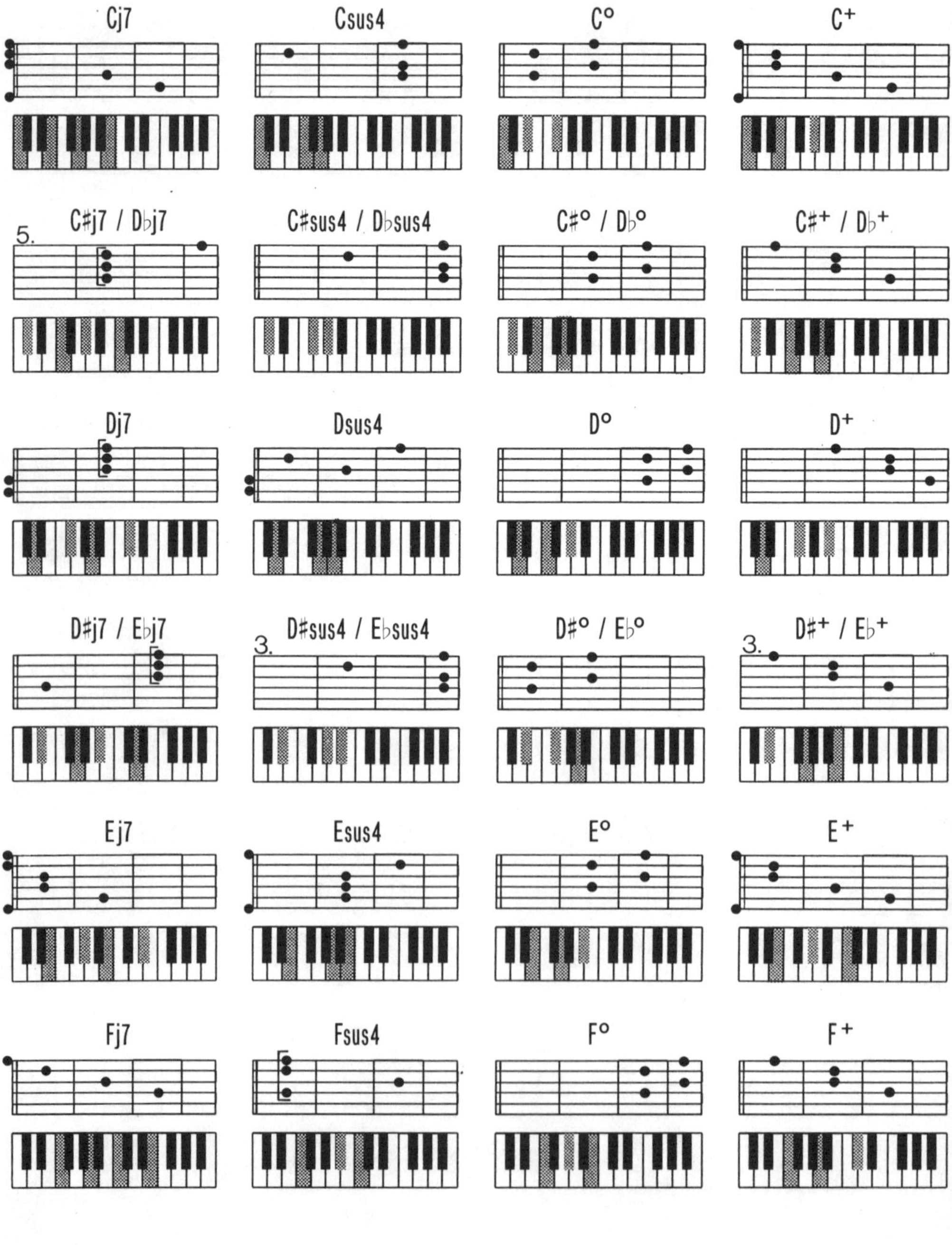

Dur^{maj7} Dur^{sus4} ° +

F♯j7 / G♭j7

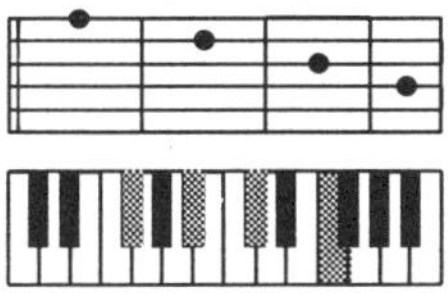

F♯sus4 / G♭sus4

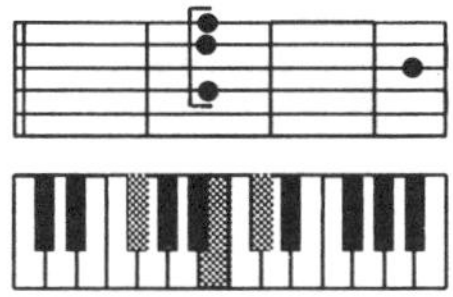

F♯° / G♭°

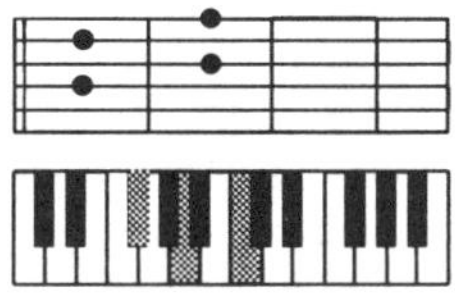

F♯$^+$ / G♭$^+$

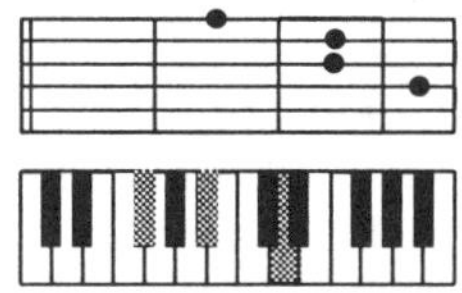

Gj7

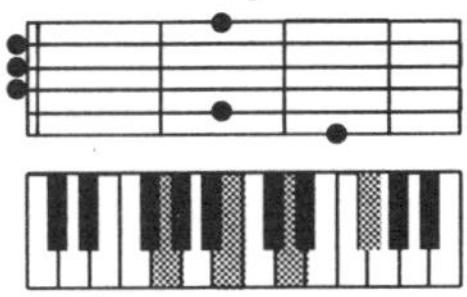

Gsus4

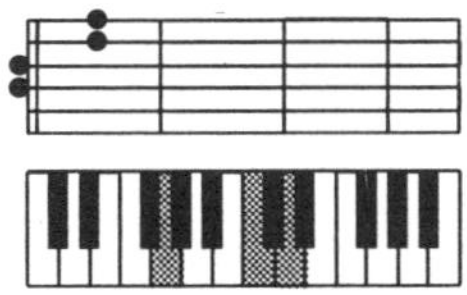

G°

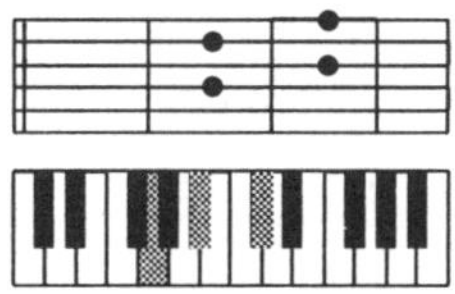

G$^+$

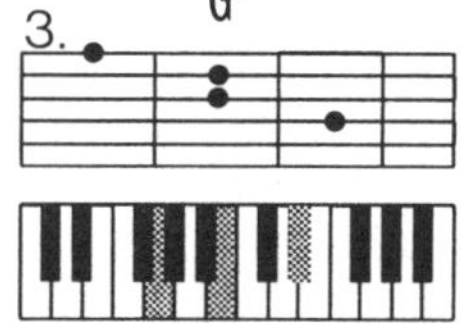

G♯j7 / A♭j7

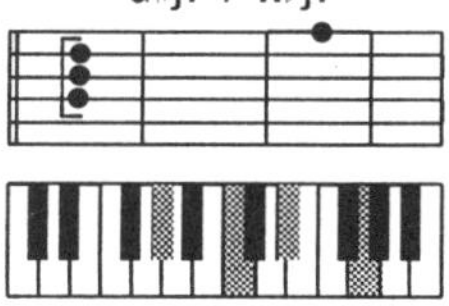

G♯sus4 / A♭sus4

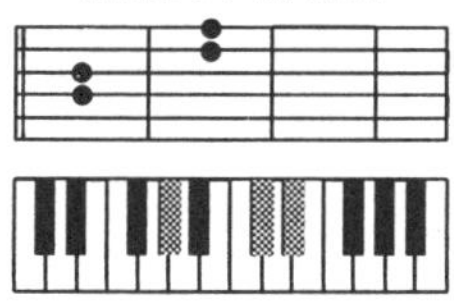

G♯° / A♭°

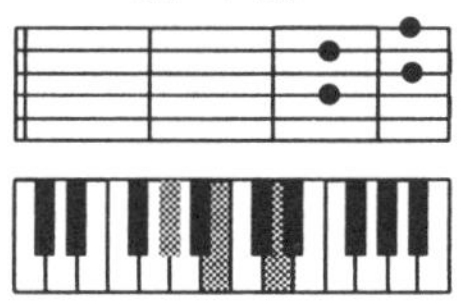

G♯$^+$ / A♭$^+$

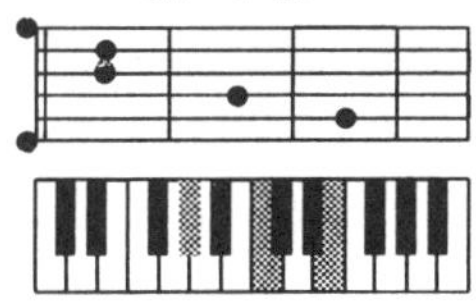

Aj7

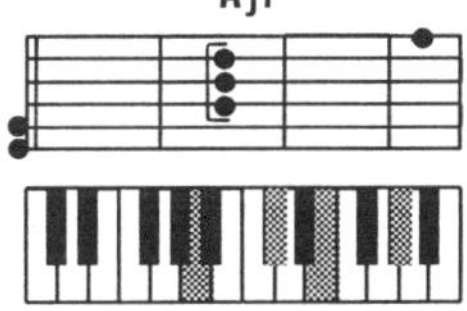

Asus4

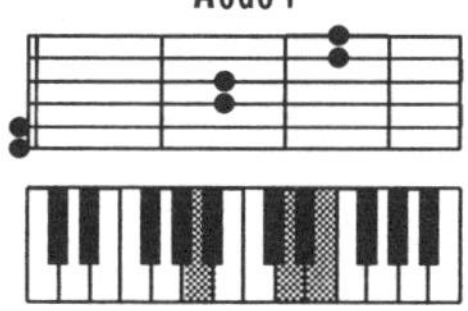

A°

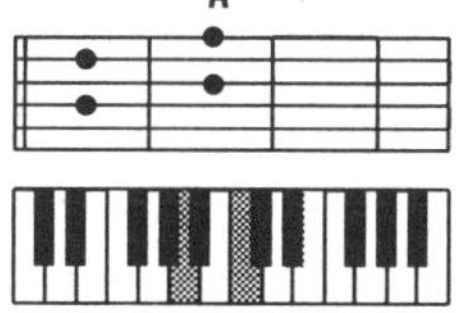

A$^+$

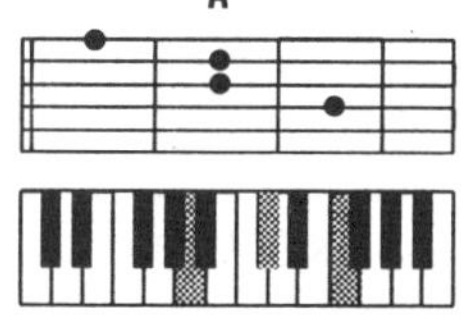

A♯j7 / B♭j7

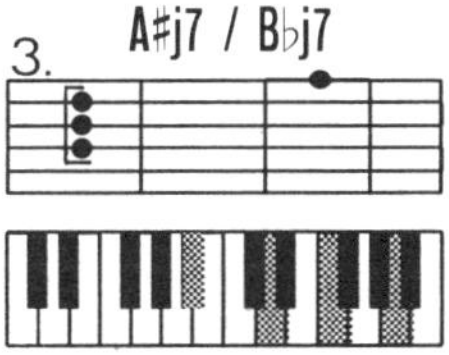

A♯sus4 / B♭sus4

A♯° / B♭°

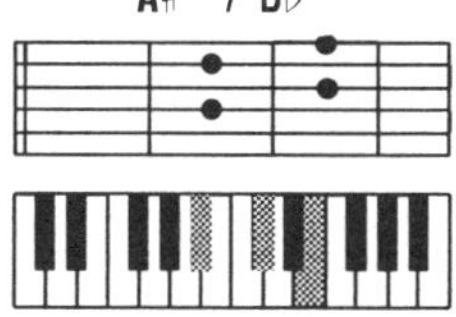

A♯$^+$ / B♭$^+$

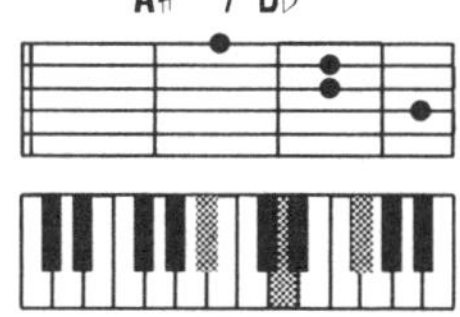

Hj7

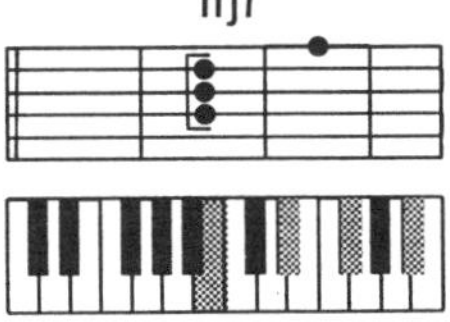

Hsus4

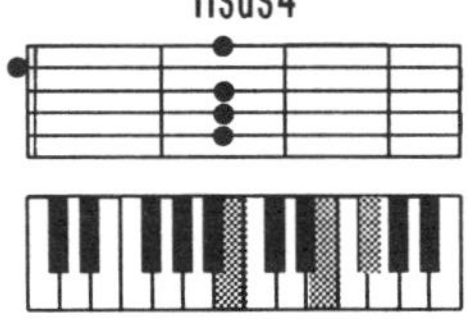

H°

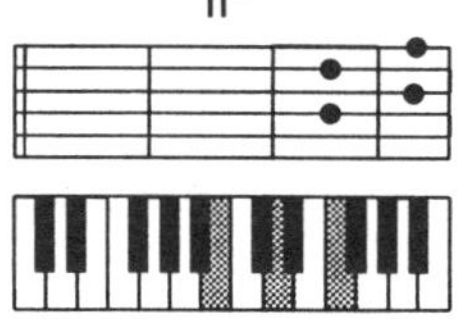

H$^+$

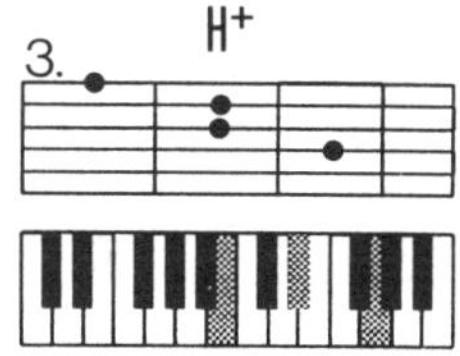

Musikbücher von KDM

Gitarre & Bass

- Kleines Gitarrenbuch
- Die wichtigsten Gitarrengriffe
- Gitarre, Band 1 und 2
- Einstieg ins Gitarrenspiel, Band 1 und 2
- Einstieg ins Gitarrenspiel – exclusiv mit CD
- Einstieg Rockgitarre mit CD
- Guidebook to Rockguitar mit CD und Poster
- Rockguitar Studioplaybacks mit 2 CDs und Poster
- Unplugged Guitar mit CD
- Modernes Fingerpicking mit CD
- Picking Classics
- Hard Rock Heavy Metal Speed Metal
  Rhythm & Lead Guitar, Band 1 mit MC
- Hard Rock Heavy Metal Speed Metal
  Rhythm Guitar, Band 2 mit MC
- Heavy Metal Guitar – Professional mit CD
- Heavy Guitar mit MC
- Bluesguitar mit CD
- Blues-Rock Guitar mit MC
- Gitarre
  Tägliche Übungen – Warm ups für Speed und Condition
- Gitarrenimprovisation
- Michael Morengas Buch der Gitarre, Band 1 mit CD
- Video zu Michael Morengas Buch der Gitarre
- Hard Rock Heavy Metal Speed Metal
  Bass Guitar mit MC

Keyboards

- Die wichtigsten Akkordgriffe für Keyboards
- Einstieg ins Keyboardspiel
- Die neue Schule für Keyboards, Band 1, 2 und 3
- Das neue Keyboardbuch, Band 1, 2 und 3 mit CD

Songbücher

- The Best Songs (diverse Bände)
- Songs & Basics (diverse Bände)
- Songbook (diverse Bände)
- The Best Oldies & Evergreens
- The Best Ballads

Basics

- Popular Drumming
- Einstieg in die Musik
- Einstieg in die Rhythmik
- Neue Musiklehre & Songcomposing
- Akkordsymbolschrift
- Einstieg ins Saxophonspiel
- Drums – Rhythm Patterns